# REALIZING INDIA'S POTENTIAL FOR TRANSIT-ORIENTED DEVELOPMENT AND LAND VALUE CAPTURE

## A QUALITATIVE AND QUANTITATIVE APPROACH

JULY 2022

ASIAN DEVELOPMENT BANK

ADB

Notes:
In this publication, "$" refers to United States dollars.
ADB recognizes "Korea" as the Republic of Korea.

Cover design by Josef Raymund Ilumin.
On the cover: The photo and graphic illustration was prepared by National Capital Region Transport Corporation (NCRTC).

# Contents

# Tables, Figures, and Boxes

**Tables**

## Figures

## Boxes

# Foreword

Transit-oriented development (TOD) is increasingly recognized as a suitable option to help address urban development issues in India. In the context of metro rail systems, it has much potential to promote inclusive and sustainable urban mobility, and enhance the livability and dynamism of cities through better integration of land use policies and development of the transport network. TOD also presents an opportunity to utilize land value capture (LVC) mechanisms to augment cities' finances.

This study seeks to understand the challenges associated with TOD implementation in selected major cities in India and how the socioeconomic benefits of TOD measures vary with land use regulations. The latter is especially important to maximize the socioeconomic benefit of investments in metro rail.

The findings of the study are presented in two sections. The first section uses existing literature and various data sources to explore the status of TOD and LVC planning and implementation in several major Indian cities and Asian cities through the lens of the planning, governance, and financing framework. Among others, a key lesson that emerges is the important role of land use management policies in determining the scope and level of socioeconomic benefits that arise from TOD.

Extending this idea, the second section of the report carries out a quantitative simulation on how relaxing floor area ratio restrictions, a key type of land use regulation, in the metro corridor can result in a multitude of city-level benefits. The results suggest that appropriate land use regulations coupled with appropriate TOD policies result in significant positive impacts on several socioeconomic outcomes and pave the way for successful implementation of land-based financing tools in metro rail projects.

As urbanization advances in India, an increasing number of Indian cities are well on track to becoming megacities. Well-integrated planning of transport investment and land use management can go a long way to realize the potential of cities.

The Asian Development Bank's Transport and Communications Division, South Asia Department and the Economic Analysis and Operational Support Division, Economic Research and Regional Cooperation Department jointly carried out this study. Liming Chen, young professional; Rana Hasan, regional economic advisor; Andri Heriawan, senior transport specialist; and Mukund Kumar Sinha, transport specialist, coordinated and supervised the study. Bouvier May Murla assisted with the production of the publication. Saugata Dasgupta, project management specialist; Kaushal Kumar Sahu, senior project officer (transport); and Sharad Saxena, principal transport specialist, provided valuable comments and technical insights on the content.

A consultant team consisting of Abhay Kantak and Gayatree Oaks from CRISIL, Ravi Ponnapureddy from the World Resource Institute (WRI), and Kala Seetharam Sridhar from the Institute for Social and Economic Change undertook the research and initial writeup. Giuseppe Tesoriere from WRI helped structure the report.

The contributors dedicate this study to the memory of Ravi Ponnapureddy, who passed away on 31 May 2021.

**Ravi Peri**
Director
Transport and Communications Division
South Asia Department

**Lei Lei Song**
Director
Economic Analysis and Operational Support Division
Economic Research and Regional Cooperation Department

# Abbreviations

| | |
|---|---|
| ADB | Asian Development Bank |
| AGR | annual growth rate |
| BBMP | Bruhat Bengaluru Mahanagara Palika |
| DLR | Deutsches Zentrum für Luft- und Raumfahrt (German Aerospace Center) |
| FAR | floor area ratio |
| FMLM | first mile and last mile |
| FSI | floor space index |
| LVC | land value capture |
| km | kilometer |
| km$^2$ | square kilometer |
| m | meter |
| MRT | mass rapid transit |
| NMT | nonmotorized transport |
| ORR | Outer Ring Road |
| PRC | People's Republic of China |
| RITES | Rail India Technical and Economic Service Limited |
| TOD | transit-oriented development |
| WRI | World Resources Institute |
| WSF | World Settlement Footprint |

# Executive Summary

India is urbanizing at a rapid pace. The level of urbanization has increased from 17.29% in 1951 to 31.6% in 2011. India's urban population, which is nearly 377 million, is projected to grow to 600 million by 2030. Considering the rapid urbanization and the imminent need for enhancing mobility in cities, it is imperative to strengthen mass transit systems and to explore alternative and innovative sources of funds to supplement budgetary resources.

Metro rail has been selected as the backbone mass transit system in many Indian cities. Most of the metro rail projects have been financed by the central government in partnership with state governments, or by state governments alone. The Government of India through its Metro Rail Policy 2017 has linked the metro rail system to the adoption of the National Transit-Oriented Development (TOD) Policy and land value capture (LVC) financing framework. The policy defines TOD as a measure to integrate land use and transport planning through the development of well-planned and sustainable urban growth centers linked with high-quality transit systems. These will support walkable and livable communities, with high-density and mixed land use, where citizens have access to open, green, and public spaces and, at the same time, will enjoy efficient transit facilities.

The Asian Development Bank (ADB) has been providing financial assistance for the development of various mass transit systems in major Indian cities. In addition to the assistance for Jaipur Metro in 2013 and Mumbai Metro in 2019, ADB has approved financial assistance to develop the Delhi–Meerut rail rapid transit system and Bengaluru Metro in 2020. ADB is currently working with the government on preparing the proposed expansion of the metro systems in Chennai and Kochi. In line with the government's Metro Rail Policy 2017, ADB seeks to strengthen the planning and implementation of TOD and LVC associated with these mass transit systems as value addition to enhance ridership and non-farebox revenue.

The purpose of this study is to understand the status of TOD and LVC planning and implementation, identify critical issues in implementing such initiatives in the Indian context, and explore how land use management policies may generate multiple socioeconomic benefits through densification.

The findings of the study are presented in two sections. The first section uses literature and various data sources to explore the status of TOD and LVC planning and implementation in several major Indian cities. The qualitative analysis in the study uses the same three-pronged approach used in a similar study by ADB in 2019 to understand the main challenges to effectively implementing TOD and LVC in India. These are

(i) planning framework:
- encouraging development and mixed-use destinations in proximity to public transit,
- improving accessibility to public transit, and
- unifying guidance for land use and transport;

(ii) governance framework:
- empowering decentralization and coordination, and
- developing mechanisms for ensuring coordination among agencies and institutions; and

(iii) financial framework:

- generating land-based revenue,
- focusing on property development as a major source for financing mass transit systems, and
- monetizing development rights where land is privately held.

To support the analysis, TOD and LVC implementation in major Asian cities are assessed and analyzed. The results call for strengthening planning, governance, and financial frameworks in Indian cities to enable the implementation of TOD and LVC.

The experiences across the cities studied suggest that land use management is a critical factor that can generate multiple positive socioeconomic benefits in the context of TOD. The second section of the report thus carries out simulations to examine how a variety of city-level outcomes are influenced by a key type of land use regulation: floor area ratio (FAR) regulations. The objective of the analysis is not to generate hard predictions, but instead to provide a quantitative sense of how city-level outcomes are influenced by the interaction of TOD and land use regulations.

The section uses data from Bengaluru to illustrate relationships between mass transit systems and land use policies. The analysis starts by comparing the urban form of Bengaluru with the urban forms in four peer cities—Hyderabad in India, Guangzhou and Shenzhen in the People's Republic of China, and Seoul in the Republic of Korea—and goes on to assess the relationship between FAR regulations and the urban form of Bengaluru. Lastly, the exercise quantifies and assesses the potential gain from relaxing FAR restrictions in the Bengaluru metro corridor under different scenarios.

To explore the urban form of the cities used in the analysis, the methodology employs a variety of remote sensing data. This reveals that between 1985 and 2015, Bengaluru and Hyderabad grew more in the outward direction, Guangzhou and Shenzhen grew both outward and upward, and Seoul grew predominantly upward. The upward expansion of Guangzhou, Shenzhen, and Seoul has led to the proliferation of high-rise and high-density buildings in these cities since the mid-1990s. In contrast, construction of tall buildings (greater than 100 meters) began only around 2007 in Bengaluru.

As part of the quantitative analysis for Bengaluru, simulations were carried out to investigate the gain from relaxing the FAR for different scenarios. The simulations show a positive impact on population and employment densities, metro ridership, property values and taxes, and jobs and wages, along with reduced emissions.

Specifically, increased FAR translates to additional residential and commercial floor space of approximately 120 million square meters. This floor space can accommodate an additional population of more than 2 million under an "open city" scenario, resulting in increased densification around metro stations. Densification, in turn, leads to direct economic benefits for the city, including about an additional 63–93 million hours of time savings and reduced carbon dioxide emissions ranging from 8,500–33,000 tons annually. Sensitivity analysis shows that safe, fast, and efficient first mile and last mile connectivity to station area is crucial for realizing the benefits estimated.

Relaxation of FAR can also contribute to wider economic benefits. By combining FAR relaxation and investment in the metro network, the simulations yield an increase of 34%–43% in aggregate property value. After accounting for the increased cost of constructing high-rise buildings, the net increase in value, if managed and distributed well, would significantly contribute to own-source revenue generation for the metro network. Econometric analysis yields an average increase in job density of approximately 3,000–5,800 jobs per square kilometer and average annual wage increases of $203–$217. The wards that benefit from increased job density host over 9% of the slum population, suggesting that improvements in accessibility and productivity would be inclusive, and not just benefit the better-off.

Taken together, the results suggest that relaxing the FAR in mass transit corridors, coupled with appropriate TOD policies, can result in a multitude of benefits including increased productivity, increased supply of new floor area, and environmental benefits. The potential increase in land values could pave the way for successful implementation of land-based financing tools for metro rail projects.

In summary, TOD and LVC can make significant contributions to the sustainability of large investments in mass transit systems, as well as the livability and economic dynamism of urban settlements. For these positive effects to be realized, however, requires establishing strong and effective planning, institutional, and financing frameworks.

# 1 Introduction

India is urbanizing at a rapid pace with the urban population rising much faster than the total population. The level of urbanization has increased from 17.3% in 1951 to 31.6% in 2011. In large urban agglomerations associated with cities such as Chennai, Delhi, and Mumbai, more than a third of the agglomeration resides outside the city's municipal limits; that population has grown at a compound annual growth rate of more than 3.5% compared with less than 1.1% for the population within municipal limits. Figure 1 plots the compound annual growth rate of core city population and that in outgrowth areas from 2001 to 2011.

## Figure 1: Population Growth Trends in Urban Agglomerations, 2001–2011

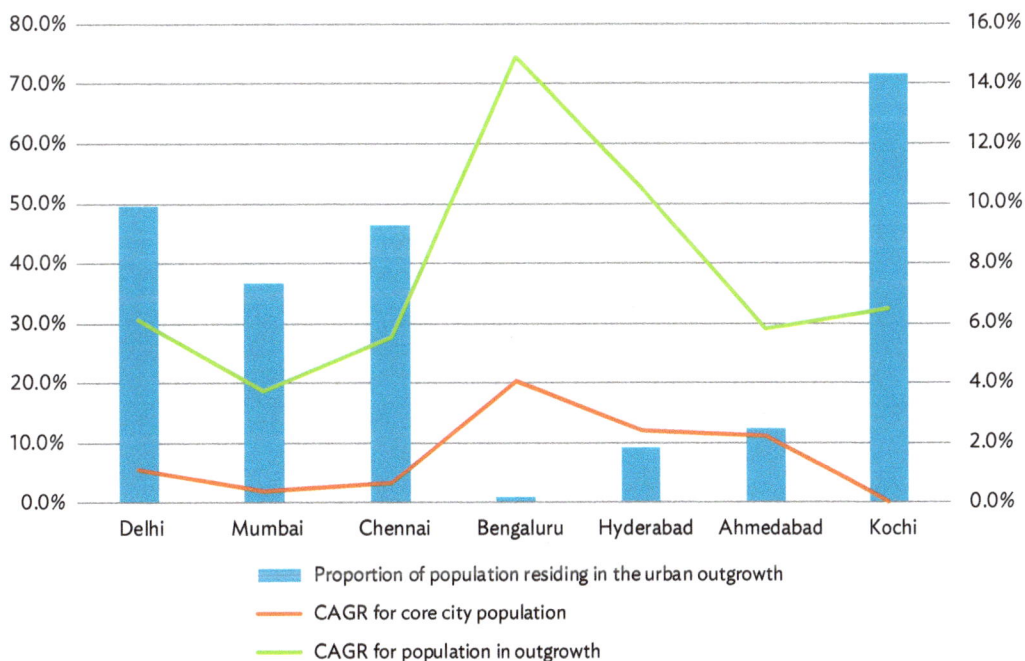

CAGR = compound annual growth rate.

Notes: Population for Delhi includes Bahadurgarh, Faridabad, Ghaziabad, Gurugram, and Noida. Population for Mumbai includes Vasai–Virar.

**Source:** Government of India, Office of the Registrar General & Census Commissioner. *2011. Census: Population Enumeration Data.* New Delhi.

Compared with cities elsewhere, Indian cities have been experiencing significantly more horizontal or outward expansion. This is evident from remote sensing data for Bengaluru, Delhi, and Hyderabad versus East Asian cities such as Seoul and Shenzhen (Figure 2).

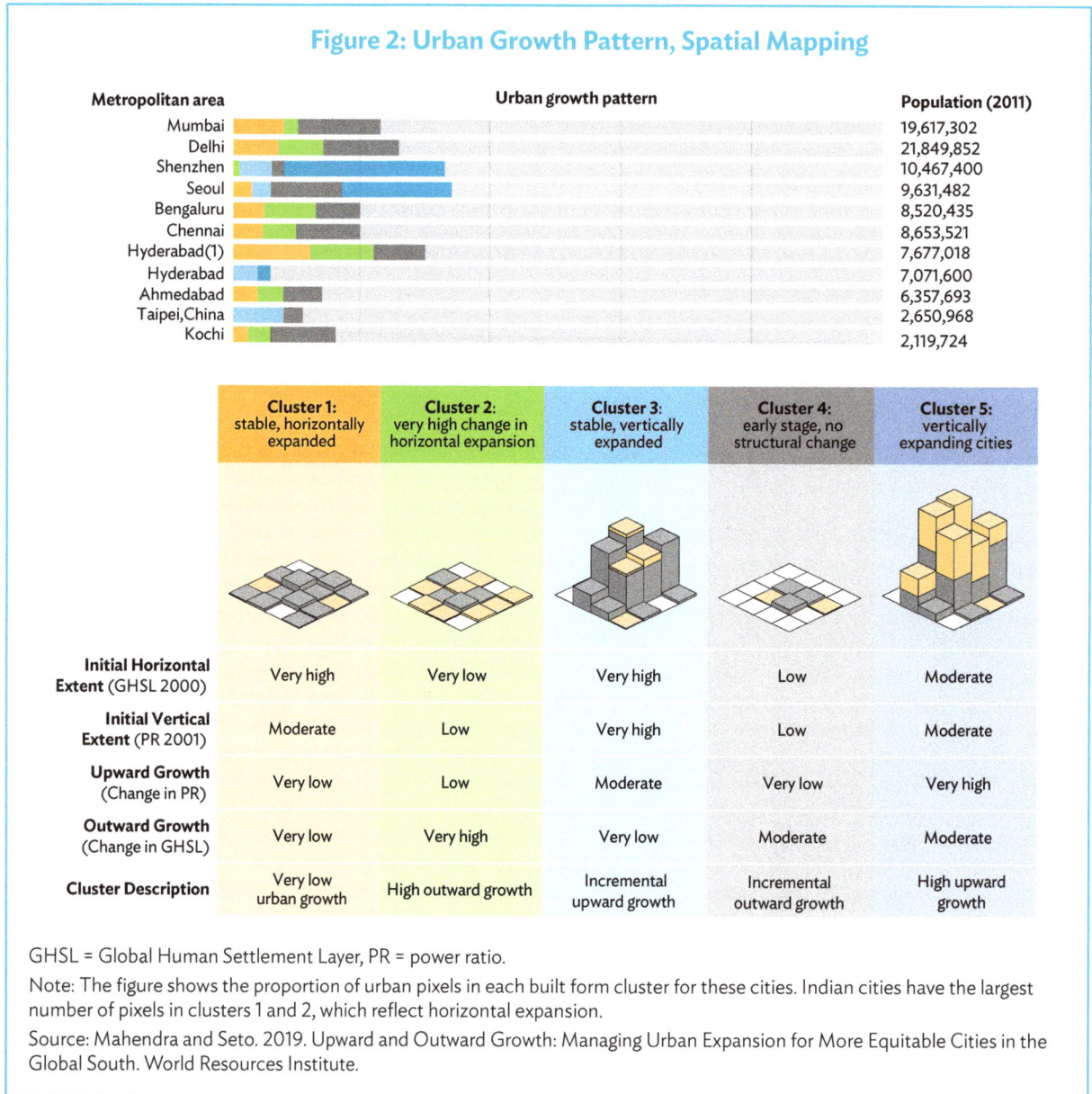

## Figure 2: Urban Growth Pattern, Spatial Mapping

| Metropolitan area | Urban growth pattern | Population (2011) |
|---|---|---|
| Mumbai | | 19,617,302 |
| Delhi | | 21,849,852 |
| Shenzhen | | 10,467,400 |
| Seoul | | 9,631,482 |
| Bengaluru | | 8,520,435 |
| Chennai | | 8,653,521 |
| Hyderabad(1) | | 7,677,018 |
| Hyderabad | | 7,071,600 |
| Ahmedabad | | 6,357,693 |
| Taipei,China | | 2,650,968 |
| Kochi | | 2,119,724 |

| | Cluster 1: stable, horizontally expanded | Cluster 2: very high change in horizontal expansion | Cluster 3: stable, vertically expanded | Cluster 4: early stage, no structural change | Cluster 5: vertically expanding cities |
|---|---|---|---|---|---|
| Initial Horizontal Extent (GHSL 2000) | Very high | Very low | Very high | Low | Moderate |
| Initial Vertical Extent (PR 2001) | Moderate | Low | Very high | Low | Moderate |
| Upward Growth (Change in PR) | Very low | Low | Moderate | Very low | Very high |
| Outward Growth (Change in GHSL) | Very low | Very high | Very low | Moderate | Moderate |
| Cluster Description | Very low urban growth | High outward growth | Incremental upward growth | Incremental outward growth | High upward growth |

GHSL = Global Human Settlement Layer, PR = power ratio.

Note: The figure shows the proportion of urban pixels in each built form cluster for these cities. Indian cities have the largest number of pixels in clusters 1 and 2, which reflect horizontal expansion.

Source: Mahendra and Seto. 2019. Upward and Outward Growth: Managing Urban Expansion for More Equitable Cities in the Global South. World Resources Institute.

To address the rapid urbanization and the imminent need for enhancing mobility, many Indian cities have strengthened their public transport by developing mass transit systems such as metro rail. Most of the metro rail projects have been financed by the central government in partnership with the state governments, or by the state governments only. Considering the need to improve mobility in cities through metro rail, it is crucial to explore new mechanisms and innovative sources of funds to supplement the budgetary resources.[1] For this reason, the

---

[1]    Government of India, Ministry of Housing and Urban Affairs. 2017. *Metro Rail Policy*. New Delhi.

Government of India through its Metro Rail Policy 2017 has linked metro rail funding to the adoption of the National Transit-Oriented Development (TOD) Policy and land value capture (LVC) financing framework.[2]

The National TOD Policy defines TOD as a measure to integrate land use and transport planning by developing well-planned and sustainable urban growth centers linked with high-quality transit systems. The policy is intended to support walkable and livable communities with high-density and mixed land use, where citizens have access to open, green, and public spaces and, at the same time, enjoy efficient transit facilities. TOD is expected to generate multiple benefits, especially in terms of sustainability, prosperity, and accessibility. In particular, TOD could play a key role in addressing critical urban issues such as urban sprawl, encouraging development within transit influence zones, and generating own-source revenue for cities from higher land values. For Indian cities, TOD calls for strengthening the institutional, planning, and financing frameworks that enable its effective implementation.

This study aims to explore the current challenges of implementing TOD in India and provides evidence on the impacts of connecting land use management with metro system planning on density and a variety of socioeconomic outcomes. The report consists of two main sections. The first consists of a qualitative analysis of TOD practices in India and other Asian economies through the lens of a three-pronged approach that focuses on planning, governance, and financial issues. This three-pronged approach was used in an ADB study in 2019, on the planning and implementation of LVC.[3] The second section considers the relationship between floor area ratio (FAR) regulations and urban form, taking Bengaluru as a case study, and quantifies the potential gain from relaxing FAR restrictions in the Bengaluru metro corridor. In this analysis, simulations across various scenarios quantify the benefits generated in the city in terms of residential shifts, agglomeration gains, travel time savings, own-source revenue generation, jobs and wages, as well as reduction in emissions.

---

[2]   Government of India, Ministry of Housing and Urban Affairs. 2017. *Transit Oriented Development (TOD) Policy*. New Delhi.
[3]   ADB. 2019. *Land Value Capture (LVC) Study*. Manila.

# 2 A Three-Pronged Approach for India's Transit-Oriented Development

This chapter follows a three-pronged approach that examines the challenges to effective implementation of TOD in terms of planning, governance, and finance issues.

(i) **Planning** looks at a holistic urban transport development approach, which integrates land use and transport planning as critical components of the TOD strategy. In essence, it explores land use planning, transport planning, and TOD elements incorporated in development control regulations and the guidelines for urban design.

(ii) **Governance** explores the roles and responsibilities allocated to various institutions involved in TOD, focusing on planning and development authorities, implementation agencies, agencies responsible for housing policies, and transport planning. Governance puts in place mechanisms that ensure a coordinated planning approach to TOD.

(iii) **Finance** focuses on the spectrum of revenue sources utilized to fund mass rapid transit (MRT) projects and TOD and investigates how TOD policies may generate own-source revenue from various land-based fiscal tools.

## Planning and Land Use

The National TOD Policy prescribes a set of key principles and recommended tools for implementing TOD. Some of the specific policy recommendations are included in Box 1.

Although the National TOD Policy has been cascaded into a state-level framework, the recommendations have been applied in various stages in Indian cities (Box 2). Most cities have not adopted the recommendations or have incorporated TOD as part of their statutory land use plans. For example, even though comprehensive TOD policies have been formulated and published in Bengaluru and Delhi as part of their development control regulations, the state-level policy in Delhi has already been finalized, whereas in Bengaluru the policy is still at the draft stage and pending the approval of the state government. In Ahmedabad, Chennai, and Hyderabad, TOD zones have been earmarked along the transit corridor under the statutory development control regulations. Meanwhile, Kochi and Mumbai have not yet incorporated TOD in their land use plans.

In general, TOD involves measures to promote higher density within TOD zones, promote socioeconomic activities, introduce provisions for public amenities and nonmotorized transport (NMT), and discourage the use of private vehicles. Implementation of such measures in Indian cities varies. The following discussions involve assessments of seven Indian cities selected for the study: Ahmedabad, Bengaluru, Chennai, Delhi, Hyderabad, Kochi, and Mumbai.

## Box 1: National Transit-Oriented Development Policy Recommendations

**Land use planning includes**

(i)  demarcation of the transit influence zone with a radius of 500–800 meters (m) from the transit station under the city's master plan and local area plans;

(ii)  provision of a minimum floor area ratio (FAR) of 300%–500% or even higher depending on size of the city in the transit influence zone, and incorporation of variations in the FAR based on factors such as infrastructure carrying capacity, transit capacity, and zoning provisions; and

(iii)  promotion of mixed-use development within the transit-oriented development (TOD) zone, with commercial activity on the ground floor and a minimum of 50% of the frontage being untinted and transparent.

**Inclusive development covers**

(i)  a minimum of 30% of the FAR to be used for affordable housing, which may be defined by the size of the tenement;

(ii)  a minimum of 10%–15% of the FAR to be developed as units for the economically weaker section, i.e., exclusively for low-income families or individuals, by providing additional FAR incentives if required; and

(iii)  designated areas to be earmarked for street vending.

**Mobility, utility Infrastructure, and amenities include**

(i)  multimodal integration, focused on pedestrian and other nonmotorized transport;

(ii)  prohibition of on-street parking within 100 m of the transit station; and

(iii)  provision of 10–12 square meters of open space per capita.

**Implementation comprises**

(i)  notification of TOD policy as part of the statutory master plan development of the city, along with necessary modifications to the building bylaws and development control regulations;

(ii)  formulation of a comprehensive plan for developing the required infrastructure within the TOD zone;

(iii)  implementation of value-capture financing through land-based taxes and charges with revenues accruing into a TOD fund set up as an escrow account;

(iv)  setting up a joint venture between the urban local body and the development authority to institutionalize planning and implementation of the TOD, with the development authority taking the lead in the interim; and

(v)  launch of awareness programs about TOD components.

Source: Government of India, Ministry of Housing and Urban Affairs. 2017. *National Transit Oriented Development (TOD) Policy*. Delhi.

---

**Box 2: Examples of Local Area Planning for Transit-Oriented Development in India**

**Provision for influence zone plans in Delhi's transit-oriented development (TOD) policy.** Under the TOD regulations, influence zone plans must be prepared for the TOD area. The plans would cover road widening (if required for infrastructure augmentation); upgrading of public streets to include multiutility zones (for peddling goods and food, parking, and service lanes); facilities for intermediate public transport, pedestrians, and nonmotorized transport; multimodal integration; and provision of public parking, urban furniture, signage, public conveniences, street vending zones, etc.

**Local area plans for the central business district (CBD) in Ahmedabad.** The Ahmedabad Urban Development Authority has used local area planning to plan for the redevelopment of the city's CBD. The identified CBD area within the influence zone of the bus rapid transit system corridor is also served by a proposed metro line. The plan proposes to increase the area under roads from 22% to 32% of the gross area while also decreasing block sizes with a finer road grid. The permissible floor area ratio (FAR) has been increased to 5.4 in lieu of the landowners paying a premium and requirements for marginal open spaces have been relaxed to assist the consumption of this higher FAR. Urban design guidelines have been framed for the area, which require maintaining an active street frontage and the location of driveways has been specified in the plan to manage vehicular conflicts.

Source: CRISIL.

---

## Promoting Higher Density within Transit-Oriented Development Zones

Indian cities have adopted a specific planning strategy for TOD, especially to increase density, develop vibrant destinations in the vicinity of transit networks, and improve accessibility to the transit systems. Density is promoted by issuing additional FAR in lieu of a monetary sum payable to the development authority or the municipal corporation. The FAR levels are typically fixed for the entire length of the transit network irrespective of the land use classification. An exception is Bengaluru, where the 2019 policy is to classify transit stations based on land use typologies such as predominantly residential, commercial, institutional, transit nodes, and others (Box 3).

---

**Box 3: Example of Density-Related Provisions
in the Transit-Oriented Development Zone, Bengaluru**

Bengaluru proposes a graded densification in the intense and general transit-oriented development (TOD) zones. Other cities in the study are not exploring such a tool. Bengaluru also allows higher floor area ratio (FARs) near transit stations for composite development (station-cum-commercial development), except in heritage zones. The city's policy states that an even higher FAR is permissible in an intense TOD zone, subject to the approval of the Detailed Development Plan or Zonal Plan of the station influence area.

The TOD policy for Bengaluru Metropolitan Region prepared in 2019 recommends that the Bengaluru Metropolitan Land Transport Authority prepare a comprehensive plan that integrates physical infrastructure and essential facilities such as roads, sewers, drainage, electric lines, green spaces, police posts, fire posts, electric substations, and others. The policy recommends evaluating the existing infrastructure's carrying capacity and upgrading it accordingly to sustain TOD.

Source: CRISIL.

While provision of an efficient and accessible transit system is an integral part of TOD, TOD is increasingly seen as a property development tool to utilize higher permissible FAR. Integration of higher FAR and accessibility to the transit system should be ensured as a prerequisite. Also, promoting higher FAR or density related to TOD requires adequate supporting infrastructure. For example, in Bengaluru and Delhi, upgrading infrastructure to sustain higher FAR is a prerequisite before permissions can be issued for developments in the TOD zone. Table 1 summarizes the provisions for increasing density along the transit network in various cities in India.

The absence of sufficient supporting infrastructure and wider scope of planning for TOD may pose greater problems. Even if FARs are relaxed, issues such as land acquisition, resettlement and reconstruction, utility management, and traffic impacts are somewhat challenging for developers to tackle alone and require support and supervision from the relevant authorities. These issues can be seen as a downside of relaxing FAR, which need careful and integrated planning process to mitigate.

### Table 1: Provisions for Increasing Density along Transit Networks

| Provision | Ahmedabad | Bengaluru | Chennai | Delhi | Hyderabad | Kochi | Mumbai |
|---|---|---|---|---|---|---|---|
| Addition over base FAR in TOD zone | 122% | 25%–50% | NA | 50% | NA | NA | NA |
| Linkage of FAR with node-place values | No | Yes | No | No | No | No | No |
| Extent of the TOD zone | 200 m | 1,000 m (around station) | 500 m (along corridor) | 500 m (around station) | 300 m (along corridor) | NA | NA |
| Provision for infrastructure augmentation | (along corridor) | Yes | No | Yes | No | No | No |

FAR = floor area ratio, m = meter, NA = not applicable, TOD = transit-oriented development.
Source: CRISIL.

While the FAR is a popular tool to promote TOD, the use of urban design interventions to promote compact development in the vicinity of transit corridors is being explored in a few places. Cities such as Bengaluru, Delhi, and Hyderabad are promoting direct access from the transit station to adjacent properties, through ramps or elevated pedestrian corridors or through physical integration of such properties with the station through joint development. In Delhi, through a cluster approach, development or redevelopment within the TOD zone is promoted in a contiguous fashion so that the population is not dispersed in pockets across the area. In Chennai, air rights above the land used for the mass transit's operation, such as transit stations, are utilized for real estate development. Table 2 summarizes the provisions to promote compact development along mass transit networks in various Indian cities.

### Table 2: Provisions for Increasing Compactness of Development along Transit Networks

| Provision | Ahmedabad | Bengaluru | Chennai | Delhi | Hyderabad | Kochi | Mumbai |
|---|---|---|---|---|---|---|---|
| Direct access from adjacent property | No | Yes | No | Yes | Yes | No | No |
| Contiguous development | No | No | No | Yes | No | No | No |
| Utilization of airspace | No | No | Yes | No | No | No | No |

Source: CRISIL.

One of the elements missing in densifying the TOD zone in this study's cities is the inclusion of socioeconomically weaker groups. Among these cities, only Bengaluru promotes the development of smaller-sized tenements in the TOD zone. The policy proposed for Bengaluru also promotes redevelopment and rehabilitation of slums in the TOD zone by providing a transfer of development rights of 30 square meters per slum household. However, measures such as securing the developing public housing stock and ensuring the development of associated amenities and facilities for such demographics remain largely unexplored in the TOD context.

## Promoting Socioeconomic Activities

Aligned with densification policies, cities have been fostering other planning strategies such as flexible zoning to promote commercial and other land use categories to ensure vibrancy in the area. For example, Ahmedabad, Bengaluru, Delhi, and Hyderabad do not limit the development of commercial activities in the TOD zone. In some of the cities, this is taken a step further with active promotion of commercial activities in the TOD zone. Bengaluru and Delhi prescribe a minimum requirement for commercial development as part of the real estate development mix in the TOD zone and identify zones where street vending is permitted (Table 3).

### Table 3: Land Use Zoning Provisions

| Provision | Ahmedabad | Bengaluru | Chennai | Delhi | Hyderabad | Kochi | Mumbai |
|---|---|---|---|---|---|---|---|
| Flexible zoning | Yes | Yes | No | Yes | Yes | No | No |
| Mandatory nonresidential development | No | Yes | No | Yes | No | No | No |

Source: CRISIL.

In Bengaluru, a minimum of 20% of the area must be allocated for commercial and institutional use. Ahmedabad and Hyderabad promote the development of office and retail complexes in the TOD zone, and Ahmedabad also encourages commercial street fronts (Table 4).

### Table 4: Commercial Development

| Development | Ahmedabad | Bengaluru | Chennai | Delhi | Hyderabad | Kochi | Mumbai |
|---|---|---|---|---|---|---|---|
| Office and retail complexes | Yes | No | No | No | Yes | No | No |
| Commercial street front | Yes | No | No | No | No | No | No |
| Street-vending, peddling zones | No | Yes | No | Yes | No | No | No |

Source: CRISIL.

## Public Amenities

Conversely, a few cities have adopted strategies for developing amenities and facilities within the TOD zone to improve the area's livability and generate trips using the mass transit systems. As seen in Table 5, this provision is most prominent in Hyderabad, followed by Ahmedabad and Delhi. Hyderabad zoning and planning regulations allow for mixed-use development in the transit-oriented zone with provision for development of residential, recreational, and commercial amenities. In Ahmedabad, the General Development Control Regulations provide for a transit-oriented zone allowing for residential, commercial, and recreational zones, which include social amenities in the form of educational structures and recreational amenities such as theaters and others. In Delhi, 20% of the area is to be developed as public open space and another 10% of open space is to be dedicated for the occupants of the development. In Chennai and Mumbai, however, the provision for public amenities is missing.

### Table 5: Provisions for Amenities

| Provision | Ahmedabad | Bengaluru | Chennai | Delhi | Hyderabad | Kochi | Mumbai |
|---|---|---|---|---|---|---|---|
| Recreation | Yes | No | No | Yes | Yes | Yes | No |
| Social amenities | Yes | No | No | Yes | Yes | No | No |
| Government offices | No | No | No | No | Yes | No | No |
| Transport facilities | No | Yes | No | No | Yes | No | No |

Source: CRISIL.

## Provision for Nonmotorized Transport

In addition to providing public amenities, there are noticeable efforts to enhance NMT around metro stations. As seen in Table 6, many of the cities have proposed improving the pedestrian and cycling infrastructure for better last mile connectivity to the metro stations. The comprehensive mobility plan for Mumbai proposes to improve pedestrian and NMT connectivity to key suburban railway stations, although such plans are also to be prepared for the metro stations. In Bengaluru, regular NMT audits have been proposed. The policy also recommends densification of NMT network to improve access to the metro stations. In Ahmedabad, bicycle network plans and complete street plans are provided in the integrated mobility plan and the development plan for the city, which have provisions for footpaths and cycling lanes. In Hyderabad, cycle tracks connecting to metro stations are proposed in the long-term strategy for the city's transport sector. However, the focus on reducing walking or cycling distance is comparatively limited.

### Table 6: Pedestrian and Nonmotorized Transport Infrastructure

| Infrastructure | Ahmedabad | Bengaluru | Chennai | Delhi | Hyderabad | Kochi | Mumbai |
|---|---|---|---|---|---|---|---|
| Footpath and cycling lanes | Yes | Yes | Yes | Yes | Yes | No | Yes |
| Cycle parking facilities | No | Yes | Yes | Yes | No | No | Yes |
| Efficient street network | No | Yes | No | Yes | No | No | No |

Source: CRISIL.

## Discouraging the Use of Private Vehicles

In line with the focus on improving NMT infrastructure, a few cities have proposed measures to discourage the use of private vehicles within the TOD zone. As seen in Table 7, Bengaluru and Delhi have proposed introducing pedestrian-only streets to discourage the use of motor vehicles. Reducing parking space as a disincentive policy for owning and using private vehicles has been proposed in Ahmedabad, Bengaluru, Chennai, and Delhi. According to the TOD policy proposed for Bengaluru, on-street parking will be prohibited within 100 m of a transit station, except for freight delivery and pickup or drop-off. On-street parking within 200 m of a metro station will be discouraged and restricted. In Ahmedabad, the private requirement allowed in the TOD zone is reduced to 35% of the total utilized FAR compared with 50% of total utilized FAR permissible in the other zones.

### Table 7: Provisions for Discouraging Private Vehicles

| Provision | Ahmedabad | Bengaluru | Chennai | Delhi | Hyderabad | Kochi | Mumbai |
|---|---|---|---|---|---|---|---|
| Nonmotorized streets | No | Yes | No | Yes | No | No | No |
| Restricted on-street parking | No | Yes | Yes | Yes | No | No | No |
| Reduced parking requirements | Yes | No | Yes | No | No | No | No |

Source: CRISIL.

# Institutions and Governance

The institutional framework for implementing TOD in India spans all three levels of government—central, state, and local—having the mandate to regulate critical functions such as planning systems, land acquisition, development of urban transport infrastructure, amenities, and utilities (Table 8). This section will briefly describe the institutional framework in the study cities.

### Table 8: Mapping of Roles and Responsibilities in Indian Cities

| | | Indian Railways | Metro Company | Bus Company | Revenue Department | Development Authority | Urban Local Body |
|---|---|---|---|---|---|---|---|
| | | Central government entity | Central and state government agency | State government agency | State government entity | State government entity | - |
| Planning | Land use | No | No | No | No | Yes | No |
| | Transport | No | No | No | No | Yes | No |
| Land acquisition | Greenfield | No | No | No | Yes | Yes | No |
| | Brownfield | No | No | No | No | No | No |
| Development | MRT | Yes | Yes | No | No | No | No |
| | Bus | No | No | Yes | No | No | Yes |
| | Roads | No | No | No | No | Yes | Yes |
| | "Intermodal integration" | No | No | No | No | No | No |
| | Amenities | No | No | No | No | Yes | Yes |
| | Housing | No | No | No | No | Yes | |
| | Commercial | Yes | Yes | No | No | Yes | Yes |
| | Utilities | No | No | No | No | No | Yes |

MRT = mass rapid transit.
Source: CRISIL.

## Planning

Planning for TOD will require the convergence of land use planning and transport planning. As summarized in Table 9, in most of the study cities, the land use plan and comprehensive transport plan are prepared by the municipal corporation and transport institutions in coordination and collaboration with development authorities. This allows the integration of land use and transport to be effectively planned and implemented.

### Table 9: Agencies Responsible for Land Use and Transport Planning: India

| | | Ahmedabad | Bengaluru | Chennai | Delhi | Hyderabad | Kochi | Mumbai |
|---|---|---|---|---|---|---|---|---|
| **Planning** | **Land use** | AUDA | BMRDA, BDA | CMDA | NCRPB, DDA | HMDA | T&CP, GCDA | MMRDA, MCGM |
| | **Transport** | AUDA | DULT, BMRCL | CMDA. CMRL | UTTIPEC, GNCTD | HMDA | KMRL, GCDA | MMRDA, MCGM |

AUDA = Ahmedabad Urban Development Authority; BDA = Bengaluru Development Authority; BMRCL = Bengaluru Metro Rail Corporation Limited; BMRDA = Bengaluru Metropolitan Region Development Authority; CMDA = Chennai Metropolitan Development Authority; CMRL = Chennai Metro Rail Limited; DDA = Delhi Development Authority; DULT = Department of Urban Land Transport; GCDA = Greater Cochin Development Authority; GNCTD = Government of National Capital Territory of Delhi; HMDA = Hyderabad Metropolitan Development Authority; KMRL = Kochi Metro Rail Limited; MCGM = Municipal Corporation of Greater Mumbai; MMRDA = Mumbai Metropolitan Region Development Authority; NCRPB = National Capital Region Planning Board; T&CP = Town and Country Planning Department, Kerala; UTTIPEC = Unified Traffic and Transportation Infrastructure (Planning and Engineering) Centre.
Source: CRISIL.

## Land Acquisition

The revenue department of the state government is responsible for allotting government land or undertaking proceedings for acquiring land from private owners under the Right to Fair Compensation and Transparency in Land Acquisition Act. Development authorities can acquire land in lieu of development rights or cash compensation, based on mutual agreement with the revenue department. Development authorities can also acquire land for public purposes through land pooling and land readjustment schemes, which are designed for greenfield land.

## Urban Transport Infrastructure

In India's urban transport sector, three tiers of the government are involved in development and operations. Metro rail development and operations are the responsibility of a special purpose vehicle jointly owned by the central and state governments. The suburban railway is run by the relevant division of the Indian Railways, which is a central government entity. Bus service is often run by the state government-owned bus transport corporation. Finally, development of urban roads and NMT is typically the responsibility of the municipal corporation. The private sector has also been engaged in developing metro projects in Hyderabad and Mumbai, where consortia led by Larsen & Toubro (for Hyderabad) and Reliance (for Mumbai) were contracted to develop the metro lines. Table 10 summarizes the agencies responsible for developing and operating transport systems in the study cities.

**Table 10: Agencies Responsible for Developing Transport Infrastructure: Indian Cities**

|  |  | Ahmedabad | Bengaluru | Chennai | Delhi | Hyderabad | Kochi | Mumbai |
|---|---|---|---|---|---|---|---|---|
| Development | Metro | GMRCL | BMRCL | CMRL | DMRC | HMRL | KMRCL | MMRDA |
|  | Rail | - | - | S. Railway | NCRTC | S. Railway | - | MRVCL |
|  | Bus | AMTS, Janmarg | BMTCL | MTC | DTC, DMRC | APSRTC | KSRTC | BEST |
|  | NMT | AUDA, AMC | BBMP | GCC | MCD | GHMC | KMTA, KMRL, CMC | MCGM |
|  | Intermodal integration | - | DULT |  | UTTIPEC | - | - | - |

AUDA = Ahmedabad Urban Development Authority, AMC = Ahmedabad Municipal Corporation, APSRTC = Andhra Pradesh State Road Transport Corporation, BBMP = Bruhat Bengaluru Mahanagara Palika, BEST = Brihanmumbai Electric Supply and Transport Undertaking, BMRCL = Bengaluru Metro Rail Corporation Limited, CMRL = Chennai Metro Rail Limited, DMRC = Delhi Metro Rail Corporation, DTC = Delhi Transport Corporation, DULT = Department of Urban Land Transport, GCC = Greater Chennai Corporation, GHMC = Greater Hyderabad Municipal Corporation, HMRL = Hyderabad Metro Rail Limited, KMRL = Kochi Metro Rail Limited, KSRTC = Kerala State Road Transport Corporation, MCD = Municipal Corporation of Delhi, MCGM = Municipal Corporation of Greater Mumbai, MMRDA = Mumbai Metropolitan Region Development Authority, MRVCL = Mumbai Rail Vikas Corporation Limited, MTC = Metropolitan Transport Corporation (Chennai) Ltd., NCRTC = National Capital Region Transport Corporation, NMT = nonmotorized transport, S. Railway = Southern Railway, UTTIPEC = Unified Traffic and Transportation Infrastructure (Planning and Engineering) Centre.
Source: CRISIL.

## Public Amenities

Public amenities for educational, health care, and recreational purposes, as well as commercial property for municipal markets and shopping complexes are usually developed by the municipal corporation within the city limit, and by the relevant development authority in the urban periphery. Residential and commercial real estate is largely supplied by private developers.

## Public Utilities

The municipal corporation is usually responsible for utility infrastructure. In cities such as Bengaluru, a state government parastatal is responsible for the city's water supply and sewerage network.

Despite this institutional framework, a clear institutional mandate to lead TOD implementation persists as a challenge. In Ahmedabad, Chennai, Delhi, and Hyderabad, the development authorities prepared the TOD policy or zoning regulations. However, the same authorities do not regulate land development or infrastructure investment in the TOD zones. Hence, implementation of the TOD schemes is entirely market-driven, with the authorities acting as regulators.

Another key challenge is the coordination mechanism. Planning is not used as a mechanism for ensuring coordinated approaches by various institutions in India. Although the institutional framework for land use planning is well-defined, there is no framework to guide transport planning and its integration with land use planning.

To fill the gap in urban transport sector planning, many Indian cities have set up a unified metropolitan transport authority. However, such institutions are not yet actively involved in transport planning and implementation. In contrast, development authorities and or metro companies prepare the mobility plans, but do not have any power to ensure that other stakeholders adhere to the plans (Table 11). However, various international agencies are supporting empowering such unified authorities and strengthening interagency coordination in urban planning.

Mass transit agencies play key roles in shaping and driving the TOD initiative forward. With financial assistance and knowledge support from ADB, the Delhi Meerut Rail Corporation and the National Capital Region Transport Corporation plan to introduce TOD-enabling schemes along the Delhi–Meerut corridor. Policy dialogue, proper dissemination of knowledge to decision makers, and strong political support from high-level officials are important to enable participation from all relevant agencies in the sectors. A similar approach is being proposed under ADB's support for Bengaluru Metro and Chennai Metro.

**Table 11: Institutions Responsible for Transport Planning and Implementation: Indian Cities**

| City | Transport Planning | |
| --- | --- | --- |
| | **Mandated institution** | **Plan prepared by** |
| Ahmedabad | – | AUDA |
| Bengaluru | BMLTA | DULT, BMRCL |
| Chennai | CUMTA | CMDA |
| Delhi | UTTIPEC | UTTIPEC, GNCTD |
| Hyderabad | UMTA | HMDA |
| Kochi[a] | – | KMRL, GCDA |
| Mumbai | UMMTA | MMRDA, MCGM |

AUDA = Ahmedabad Urban Development Authority, BMRCL = Bengaluru Metro Rail Corporation Limited, BMLTA = Bengaluru Metropolitan Land Transport Authority, CMDA = Chennai Metropolitan Development Authority, CUMTA = Chennai Urban Metropolitan Transport Authority, DULT = Department of Urban Land Transport, GCDA = Greater Cochin Development Authority, GNCTD = Government of National Capital Territory of Delhi, HMDA = Hyderabad Metropolitan Development Authority, KMRL = Kochi Metro Rail Limited, MCGM = Municipal Corporation of Greater Mumbai, MMRDA = Mumbai Metropolitan Region Development Authority, UMMTA = Unified Mumbai Metropolitan Transport Authority, UMTA = Unified Metropolitan Transport Authority, UTTIPEC = Unified Traffic and Transportation Infrastructure (Planning and Engineering) Centre.

[a] The Kochi Metropolitan Transport Authority (KMTA) has been recently set up. However, this institution did not exist at the time the comprehensive mobility plan was prepared by Kochi Metro Rail Limited.

Source: CRISIL.

# Finance and Funding Mechanisms

Funding metro rail projects in India has been "a mixed bag"—comprising private and central and state government investments. Under the Metro Rail Policy 2017, the government has linked its financial assistance to state and local agencies for metro projects to their adoption of the National TOD Policy and the LVC financing framework (Box 4).

Most of the mass transit projects in the study cities are financed through 50:50 joint ventures between central and state governments. Equity is contributed by the central or state governments, but any debt for the metro projects is expected to be repaid through internal accruals of the metro company. The metro lines in Hyderabad and Mumbai are examples of metro projects developed through a public–private partnership model. In Delhi, a 22.7-kilometer metro line connecting the city to the airport was initially developed through public–private partnership and opened in 2011. However, Delhi Metro Rail Corporation took the project over from the private operator in 2013. A network of more than 130 km of metro lines being developed in Mumbai by the Maharashtra government is an example of a fully state-funded metro project. Table 12 lists the modes of implementation of metro rail projects in the study cities.

---

**Box 4: Metro Rail Policy 2017 at a Glance**

The Metro Rail Policy 2017 provides guidance on the planning and implementation of metro rail projects. Policy prescriptions related to transit-oriented development (TOD), land value capture (LVC), transport planning, and project development include

 (i) preparing a comprehensive mobility plan, which is a mandatory prerequisite for planning a metro rail and accessing central financial assistance;

 (ii) setting up a unified metropolitan transport authority as a statutory body tasked with planning, coordination, and financing of urban transport is a mandatory prerequisite for accessing central financial assistance; and

 (iii) requiring urban local bodies or development authorities to have a stake in the agencies responsible for the metro rail.

Points to be considered in project development for a metro rail are

 (i) achieving cost recovery of the utility infrastructure investments for densifying areas around transit corridors through the project itself;

 (ii) providing feeder systems for the transit stations through a combination of paratransit modes, pedestrian, and other nonmotorized transport infrastructure to ensure the catchment extends to at least 5 kilometers from the transit station;

 (iii) mandating adoption of the national guidelines on TOD;

 (iv) mandating adoption of LVC with a mechanism for direct transfer of financial benefits arising from TOD zones to the metro rail special purpose vehicle; and

 (v) commercial development of stations and other land allocated to the special purpose vehicle.

Overall, the policy proposes the following models under which metro rail projects would be eligible for central financial assistance:

 (i) central government support by way of viability gap funding for public–private partnership projects;

 (ii) central government grant to the state government, of 10% of project cost, excluding private investment and cost of land, rehabilitation and resettlement, and tax; and

 (iii) an equity sharing model under which central and state governments share equity equally.

Source: Government of India, Ministry of Housing and Urban Affairs. 2017. *Metro Rail Policy*. Delhi.

---

In general, the cities have made limited use of LVC for financing mass transit systems. Land-based tax revenues accruing to the central government include capital gains tax on the sale of property, income tax, and goods and services tax on rented property. For the state government, the only land-based tax revenue is the stamp duty, which accrues mainly in urban areas. Other land-based taxes and charges, such as premium FAR, development charges, and property tax, only accrue to development authorities and urban local bodies (Box 5).

The only nontax, land-based revenue that the central or state government can access is the monetization of their own land assets. In some cases, metro agencies are allocated government land to augment their financial resources. However, the extent of allocated lands is limited. Innovations in property development include adopting a joint development model for transit stations in Bengaluru and using airspace above mass rapid transit (MRT) stations proposed in Chennai; a similar approach has also been undertaken in Navi Mumbai. These practices, however, have yet to find wider adoption.

### Table 12: Implementation Mode for Metro Rail: Indian Cities

| City | Length of Operational and Under-Construction Metro Network (km) | | | |
| --- | --- | --- | --- | --- |
| | Public–Private Partnership | Joint Venture (Central and State Governments) | State Government-Funded | Total |
| Ahmedabad | 0.0 | 68.3 | 0.0 | 68.3 |
| Bengaluru | 0.0 | 114.3 | 0.0 | 114.3 |
| Chennai | 0.0 | 53.3 | 0.0 | 53.3 |
| Delhi | 0.0 | 348.7 | 0.0 | 348.7 |
| Hyderabad | 72.0 | 0.0 | 0.0 | 72.0 |
| Kochi | 0.0 | 27.2 | 0.0 | 27.2 |
| Mumbai | 11.4 | 33.5 | 130.2 | 175.1 |

Source: CRISIL.

---

#### Box 5: Property Development for Financing Mass Rapid Transport: Bengaluru, Delhi, Hyderabad, and Kochi

For Delhi Metro Rail Corporation, revenue from property development is estimated to cover the following shares of the capital cost for the metro phases: 7.0% for phase I, 5.6% for phase II, and 7.3% for phase III. Hyderabad is implementing the metro on a rail+property model where L&T Metro Rail (Hyderabad) Ltd. is allotted about 109 hectares (269 acres) of land, in which L&T is allowed to develop about 12.5 million square feet (ft$^2$) at terminal locations and 6 million ft$^2$ adjoining metro stations as joint development.[a]

In Kochi, "brownfield property development" was initiated where the public works department of Kochi demolished dilapidated nongovernment organization quarters at Kakkanad and handed the property over to Kochi Metro Rail Ltd. for commercial development.

An example of joint development in Bengaluru is the IKEA store development connected to the Nagasandra metro station. IKEA has acquired about 5.6 hectares (14 acres) on a long-term lease of 60 years from Bengaluru Metro Rail Corporation Ltd. to develop about 0.45 million ft$^2$ for a store that would be connected to the Nagasandra metro station for easy access by passengers.[b]

[a] 12.5 million ft$^2$ is about 1.16 million m$^2$, and 6 million ft$^2$ is about 557,000 m$^2$.
[b] 0.45 million ft$^2$ is about 42,000 m$^2$.
Sources: L&T Metro Rail (Hyderabad) Ltd, Detailed Project Report for Hyderabad Metro Rail - Phases I, II, and III.

---

Although the Metro Rail Policy 2017 recommends that municipal corporations or development authorities have a stake in the metro project, this is not typically implemented. By requiring development authorities and municipal corporations to invest in mass transit projects, the institutions could have been encouraged to align themselves with TOD initiatives and help recover their investments through the LVC mechanism.

An alternative is to earmark a surcharge on taxes and charges or a portion of the existing taxes for accrual to agencies developing mass transit projects. In Gujarat, Karnataka, and Maharashtra, there are proposals to allow for a surcharge on development charges and part of the premium FAR collected by development authorities and municipal corporations to be earmarked for mass transit investments. These resources would need to be periodically transferred by the development authorities and municipal corporations, and do not automatically accrue to the metro development agencies. In the absence of clear governance, accounting, and transfer of these resources, or an escrow mechanism, the availability of these resources for mass transit investments is uncertain.

Under the existing frameworks, TOD in the Indian context is primarily designed to be market-driven. This means that the planning authority creates the development regulations and waits for the market to respond, mostly leveraging private sector real estate investments.

The dependence on private investments is not only to directly finance the property development, but also supporting infrastructure through payment of premium on the additional FAR or FAR and development charges. In Delhi, the private developer is expected to finance the cost of TOD under the policy. Additional FAR and TOD charges are expected to be levied on the developer under this policy. The additional FAR charges would accrue to the municipal corporation to augment infrastructure, while revenue from TOD charges would be deposited in the respective node's ring-fenced TOD fund. A committee will be set up under the chairpersonship of the lieutenant governor of Delhi comprising representatives from the Delhi Development Authority. Various service providing agencies and all local bodies would be responsible for approving any expenditure from the TOD fund.

Despite this development regulation, the land-based fiscal tools are not well linked to the market value of land in Indian cities (Table 13). State governments typically maintain a guideline for land values for the purpose of levying stamp duty. The guideline for land value is periodically revised based on information from actual real estate transactions and treated as the official government prices for land. While in many cases the premium to be charged on additional FAR has been linked to this guideline, property tax and development charge are not. Among the cities being studied, only in Mumbai are the development charge and property tax linked to the official government rates for the market value of property.

### Table 13: Taxes and Charges Linked to Market Value of Land: Indian Cities

| City | Development Charge | Property Tax | Taxes or Charges Linked to Market Value of Property | | |
|------|------|------|------|------|------|
| | | | Additional FAR | Betterment Levy | Stamp Duty |
| Ahmedabad | No | No | Yes | Yes | Yes |
| Bengaluru | No | No | Yes | Yes | Yes |
| Chennai | No | No | Yes | Yes | Yes |
| Delhi | No | No | Yes | Yes | Yes |
| Hyderabad | No | No | No | Yes | Yes |
| Kochi | No | No | No | Yes | Yes |
| Mumbai | Yes | Yes | Yes | Yes | Yes |

FAR = floor area ratio.
Source: CRISIL.

# 3 Lessons from Major Asian Cities

## Planning: Encouraging the Development and Mixed-Use Destinations Near Public Transit

Evidence from practices in major Asian cities suggests that a standard mechanism to integrate land use management with transport planning, including TOD, involves institutional strengthening and suitable regulatory provisions. Key evidence from the planning point of view is provided below.

### Encouraging Development Near Public Transit

Relaxing floor space regulations along transit corridors is used to encourage developers to invest in property development along the corridors (Box 6).

---

**Box 6: Densification Strategies: Singapore; Taipei,China; and the People's Republic of China**

**Densification of transit corridors as an urban development strategy.** In Singapore, transit lines have been consistently aligned with high-density development corridors since the first concept plan prepared in 1971. In 2003, floor space regulations around select transit stations were relaxed to double the original value to attract private investments to promote redevelopment and ensure a more intensive use of the land.

**Varying the permissible floor space according to node potential.** In 2019, Taipei,China promoted development around 33 transit stations by relaxing floor space regulations for developments within 300 meters of the station. The extent of the incentive is linked to the proximity to the station and the functional hierarchy of the station.

**Promoting development along transit corridors while discouraging development in other areas.**
The People's Republic of China's national transit-oriented development (TOD) policy recommends setting a minimum floor area ration (FAR) in the TOD zone, while also limiting the FAR outside the TOD zone to 60% of the minimum floor area ratio set in the TOD zone.

Sources: Urban System Studies. 2018. Centre for Livable Cities (CLC), Singapore; Taipei,China's TOD Policy 2019; *Guidelines for Planning and Design of Areas Along Urban Rail for People's Republic of China*, 2015.

---

## Creating Destinations Near Public Transit

Developing public amenities and facilities or commercial nodes in the vicinity of public transit would help attract commuters while ensuring that the facilities are accessible to a larger portion of the population (Box 7). This initiative, also called "placemaking," is expected to bring socioeconomic benefits and vibrance to the area, and to attract investments in the long term.

### Box 7: Developing Destinations around Transit Stations: Taipei,China; Singapore; and Hong Kong, China

**Setting up individual tertiary amenities and shopping complexes adjacent to transit stations.** Taipei,China's transit-oriented development (TOD) policy recommends prioritizing a core area of 300–500 meters (m) around transit stations for commercial centers and community-level facilities. It also recommends that commercial nodes be developed at the interchange of at least two transit corridors. The Zhongshan and East Metro malls in Taipei,China have been developed underground alongside the transit line. Zhongshan mall is 815 m long stretching across the metro stations in the city of Taipei,China; Zhongshan; and Shuanglian. The East Metro is 725 m long and stretches across Zhongxiao Fuxing station to Zhongxiao Dunhua station. The two malls together house 186 shops.

In Singapore, an 800 m long and 30 m wide pedestrianized street with an underground mall has been proposed to link Thomson–East Coast Line's Marina South and Gardens by the Bay mass rapid transit (MRT) stations. In Singapore, the Ng Teng Fong General Hospital and Jurong Community Hospital have been strategically located right across the Jurong East MRT station and bus interchange.

**Development of transit stations as integrated transport hubs.** Nine transit stations in Singapore have been developed with air-conditioned bus interchanges integrated with the stations and complemented with shopping avenues. Another 11 such hubs have been planned at Beauty World, Bedok South, Bidadari, Buangkok, Hougang, Jurong East, Marina South, Pasir Ris, Punggol North, Tampines North, and Tengah.

The TOD policy in Taipei,China mandates that transit stations and intercity transport hubs be developed not more than 500 m from each other.

**Development of transit stations as mixed-use complexes.** The Bedok Town Center in Singapore is planned as an integrated transport hub. It includes private residential housing, commercial development, a pedestrian mall, and a shopping mall. The hub is being integrated with the Bedok MRT station and an air-conditioned bus interchange.

In Hong Kong, China, the Maritime Square shopping center (with over 46,000 square meters of retail space) has been developed with seamless integration to the Tsing Yi Station and the development above and alongside the station, which includes a residential development, open space, and recreational facilities.

Source: CRISIL

## Improving Accessibility to Public Transit

In addition to encouraging people to live near transit stations and develop destinations in the area, it is important that people can easily and comfortably access these places, such as by walking or cycling from the transit station (Box 8).

---

### Box 8: Improving Access to Transit Stations: The People's Republic of China and Singapore

**The People's Republic of China's transit-oriented development policy**

**Dense road network.** The policy proposes a road network density of at least 6–8 kilometers per square kilometer, while limiting road width to 20 meters (m). Furthermore, the recommendation is that the sides of neighborhood blocks should not exceed 200 m long, and less than 120 m in transit-oriented development (TOD) zones in the city center.

**Disincentivizing private vehicles.** Parking requirements in the TOD area are to be 15%–20% of that beyond the area.

**Intermodal connections.** The stations are to be planned as multimodal nodes with parking facilities for buses, bicycles, and cars. The nature of parking facilities to be provided is to be linked to the level of traffic served by the metro line and the hierarchy of the station.

**Direct integration with adjacent plots.** Based on the hierarchy of the station, guidance is provided on the nature of pedestrian integration with the adjoining development.

**Singapore initiatives**

**Sheltered walkways.** In Singapore, 150 kilometers of covered link-ways between mass rapid transit (MRT) stations, residential areas, and amenities have been proposed for completion by 2040, including sheltered walkways between transport nodes such as MRT and light rail transit stations, bus interchanges, bus shelters, and the neighboring amenities such as centers for peddlers and commercial buildings.

**Cycling facilities.** Bicycle parking facilities are provided at MRT station exits. Private developers with property in the vicinity of MRT stations are required to submit walking and cycling plans to ensure that their property does inhibit access to the stations by people using Namtiali Railway Station.

Source: CRISIL

---

## Developing Unified Guidance for Land Use and Transport Developments

Given that TOD involves the convergence of land use and transport developments, a combined land use and transport plan or policy should be prepared to inform the development direction in these sectors (Box 9).

## Integrating Mass Transit Development with Financial Planning, Land Use Planning, and Urban Design

To ensure successful outcomes, the design of mass transit projects must be financially viable and supported through compatible land use and urban design interventions. To this end, land use regulations and plans need to be reviewed while developing a mass transit project, with station-level assessment so that any changes needed in the plans for achieving synergy with the mass transit system can be identified (Box 10).

TOD requires a complex institutional framework to regulate land use, transit, and private sector investments. Empowering decentralized institutions and strengthening coordination mechanisms between them are required. Key evidence in strengthening institutional capacity and governance in the Asian context is provided in Boxes 9 and 10.

---

### Box 9: Unified Guidance for Land Use and Transport: The People's Republic of China and Singapore

**Comprehensive transit-oriented development policy.** The People's Republic of China issued a national-level TOD policy in 2015. It lays out transit-oriented development (TOD) considerations at three levels. At the city level, the policy provides guidance on incorporating TOD into urban planning with respect to floor area ratio control, road network design, and alignment of spatial growth with the transit network. At the corridor level, it provides guidance on the alignment of metro lines, location of transit stations, intermodal linkages, and land use in the vicinity of transit stations. Finally, at the site level, it prescribes the framework for evaluating property development, integrating transit stations with adjacent properties, and designing urban guidelines for pedestrian infrastructure.

**Integrated land use and transport planning.** While Singapore does not have a dedicated policy document or directive on TOD, the guidance is formulated through a concept plan that provides centralized guidance on land use and transport for Singapore. Five key government agencies are involved in preparing the concept plan. The Land Transport Authority is in charge of all land transport matters, while the Urban Redevelopment Authority is the central city planner. The Housing Development Board plans housing estates or towns, the Jurong Town Corporation develops industrial and business parks, and the National Parks Board is in charge of making Singapore a city in a garden. Drawing from this concept plan, the Urban Redevelopment Authority prepares the statutory land use master plan, while the Land Transport Authority prepares the Land Transport Master Plan.

Source: CRISIL.

---

### Box 10: Integrating Mass Rapid Transit Project Development with Financial Planning, Land Use Planning, and Urban Design: Hong Kong, China

MTR Corporation Limited (MTRC), Hong Kong, China, incorporates a review of the land use regulation based on an assessment of the real estate market while undertaking property development along the transit rail. Tung Chung and Tseung Kwan O are two cases where the MTRC approached the Town Planning Board and submitted an application for changes in the prescribed land use. In the case of Tung Chung, the MTRC's intervention pertained to the scale of the project and urban design. In the case of Tseung Kwan O, the MTRC assessed the proposal on land use zoning to develop the land as an office building as being impractical. The MTRC also identified the diminished demand for shopping given the oversupply in the vicinity. Instead, the MTRC proposed an application to allow development of residences and hotels. This approach of reviewing the land use of property adjacent to a transit station based on an assessment of the real estate market, as well as planning and design considerations, has also been adopted in in Shenzhen, People's Republic of China.

Source: CRISIL 3.2. Governance: Empowering Decentralization and Coordination

# Empowering Agencies Responsible for Transit System Development and Operation

Agencies responsible for developing and operating transit systems are well-positioned to lead the adoption of TOD initiatives and need to be empowered to do so, particularly as a means to recover large capital investments in mass transit systems and increase ridership (Box 11). However, their focus on TOD is still limited to properties in the immediate vicinity of the transit stations or specific parcels of land allocated to them. Beyond these, their role is usually restricted to providing last mile connectivity through NMT or paratransit.

---

### Box 11: Transit Authorities Leading Transit-Oriented Development: Taipei,China and Hong Kong, China

The Department of Rapid Transit (DORT) in Taipei,China, which is responsible for developing the transit infrastructure, is also responsible for developing the property around the metro stations under a joint development model. Under the Mass Rapid Transit Act, the DORT is assigned the mandate of land development, including plots occupied by the transit infrastructure and the rest of the block where these facilities are located. Underground or overground linkages may also cover neighboring blocks. Thus, the DORT is able to influence control over this larger area and undertake transit-oriented development (TOD) through joint development schemes. These joint development schemes, however, do not cater to TOD opportunities beyond the extent of a block, and the DORT does not necessarily undertake joint development at all transit stations. Therefore, the Department of Urban Development formulated a policy in 2019 to promote TOD in such areas.

In Hong Kong, China, the Metro Transit Rail Corporation (MTRC) acts as the master planner and designer and, thus, is able to propose changes to the land use plans and regulatory zoning. This allows the MTRC to mainstream TOD considerations into the planning process by routing metro lines in urban areas with real estate potential, or by planning for the development that will fuel ridership in the future. While the MTRC can make a case for changes to the land use plans and regulations, the town planning board needs to approve them.

Source: CRISIL

---

# Empowering Institutions Responsible for Land Use Planning and Land Development

Empowering institutions responsible for land use planning and land development is required because these institutions cater to socioeconomic development along the transit corridors, which is closely related to the LVC objectives (Box 12). Therefore, it is essential that these institutions consider the TOD initiatives as a core urban development strategy, and the institutions should be oriented to attract private sector investments. Collaborative efforts are required between land use authorities and transport authorities.

### Box 12: A Land Use Planning Authority Leading Transit-Oriented Development: Singapore

In Singapore, transit-oriented development (TOD) is largely led by the Urban Redevelopment Authority (URA), which dons multiple hats, as it is responsible for land use planning and urban redevelopment, and it is one of the key agents for leasing government land. This allows the URA to create livable and dense development along the transit corridors, while also focusing on maximizing the land value capture potential via land sales. Being the land use regulator, the URA is also enabled to ensure that the development facilitates nonmotorized transport and is well-integrated with transit stations. The URA is supported by the Land Transport Authority (LTA), which is responsible for developing transit lines. The LTA was responsible for demonstrating the technical viability of the first integrated commercial development using airspace above the Dhoby Ghaut Nel station, which was designed as a five-level interchange station. The LTA also prepared a set of detailed guidelines for the integration of properties with the transit station to ensure that it does not affect the transit operations or pose safety concerns.

Source: Centre for Liveable Cities. 2018. *Urban System Studies*. Singapore.

## Empowering Institutions Responsible for Promoting Economic Development

Institutions that are responsible for promoting economic development are better positioned to lead TOD than institutions that have a regulatory relationship with the private sector (Box 13).

### Box 13: An Economic Development Authority Leading Transit-Oriented Development: Shenzhen

In Shenzhen, the Municipal Development and Reform Commission is responsible for structuring the rail+property model for transit-oriented development so that it optimizes economic as well as social objectives. The commission prepares the short-term plan for rail transit, working with the metro companies, and the municipal departments are responsible for scouting for project development land sites and for revisiting planning parameters and metro routes. However, as a safeguard, the Municipal Planning and Natural Resources Board retains the final decision over the plan. Also, the metro company is responsible for executing transit-oriented development by developing the allocated lands.

Source: Government of Shenzhen. http://www.sz.gov.cn/en.

Decentralization is overwhelmingly suggested across the case studies. Nonetheless, the complexity of the TOD system necessitates a proper mechanism to ensure good coordination between institutions, especially between agencies responsible for land use and land development, those responsible for transport, and the private sector (Box 14).

Table 14 summarizes the roles and responsibilities of major stakeholder organizations in five Asian cities.

---

**Box 14: Coordination between Land Use and Transport Agencies:
Singapore; Shenzhen; and Taipei,China**

**Integrated planning.** Singapore has a practice of formulating a centralized concept plan prepared collaboratively by five key agencies: the Land Transport Authority, Urban Redevelopment Authority, Housing Development Board, Jurong Town Corporation, and National Parks Board. This enables collaboration and coordination from the planning stage. In Shenzhen, the Municipal Planning and Natural Resources Bureau responsible for land use planning is also empowered to approve the transport plan prepared by the Municipal Transport Bureau, and the short-term rail transit plan prepared by the Development and Reform Commission.

In Taipei,China, proposals for transit-oriented development projects are subject to the approval of a working committee constituting the Taipei,China's Government Metropolitan Development Bureau, Finance Bureau, Department of Rapid Transit, Transportation Bureau, Industrial Development Bureau, Urban Renewal Office, and other related units.

**Representation on the board.** The chief executive officer of the Land Transport Authority responsible for land transport in Singapore is a member of the board of the Urban Renewal Authority responsible for implementing transit-oriented development through land use planning and property development.

**Setting up a dedicated coordination cell.** In Shenzhen, an urban transit rail office has been set up under the mayor to coordinate between the various stakeholders.

Source: CRISIL

---

**Table 14: Roles and Responsibilities of Stakeholders in Major Asian Cities**

| | | Hong Kong, China | Seoul | Shenzhen | Singapore | Taipei,China |
|---|---|---|---|---|---|---|
| Planning | Transport | Transport department | CTO | MTB | LTA | DOT |
| Development | Metro | MTRC | Seoul Metro | SMRC | LTA | DORT |
| | Bus | Transport department | CTO | MTB | LTA | DOT |
| | NMT | Transport department | CTO | MTB | LTA, URA | DOT |
| | Intermodal | Transport department | CTO | MTB | LTA | DOT |
| O&M | Metro | MTRC | Seoul Metro and Metro 9 | SMRC | SMRT, SBS Transit | TRTC |
| | Bus | Transport department | CTO | MTB | SMRT, SBS Transit | DOT |

CTO = City Transport Office of Seoul Municipal Government, DORT = Department of Rapid Transit, DOT = Department of Transportation, LTA = Land Transport Authority, MTB = Municipal Transport Bureau of Shenzhen Municipal Government, MTRC = MTR Corporation Ltd, O&M = operations and maintenance, SMRC = Shenzhen Metro Rail Corporation, SMRT = SMRT Corporation, TRTC = Rapid Transit Corporation Metro Service, URA = Urban Redevelopment Authority.
Source: CRISIL.

# Finance: Generating Land-Based Revenue

The funding strategies for building metro rail vary across the Asian cities (Table 15 and Box 15). Government capital grants play a primary role. The grants received from the government may be an indirect source of LVC—drawing from land sales by other public institutions and proceeds for land-based taxes.

### Table 15: Source of Metro Rail Funding in Asian Cities

| City | Metro Company | Government Capital Grant | Property Development |
|------|---------------|-------------------------|----------------------|
| Hong Kong, China | Yes | Yes | Yes |
| Seoul | No | Yes | No |
| Shenzhen | Yes | No | Yes |
| Singapore | No | Yes | No |
| Taipei,China | No | Yes | Yes |

Source: CRISIL.

---

### Box 15: Land-Based Revenue as Key Sources: Singapore and Taipei,China

Singapore and Taipei,China largely use government grants for financing mass rapid transit development.

- Revenue from land sales in Singapore was about $11,663 million in fiscal year 2017 and $10,982 million in fiscal year 2018. That is 88% of total development expenditure in 2017 and 73% in 2018. Also, proceeds from property tax were about $3,285 million in 2017 and $3,397 million in 2018.
- Land-based taxes such as land value tax, land value increment tax, and house tax comprised 77.5% of Taipei,China's tax revenue in 2019.

Sources: Statistics on revenue collection, Department of Finance, Taipei,China City Government; Revenue and expenditure estimates, Ministry of Finance, Singapore.

---

Key evidence from financing in the Asian context is provided below.

## Focusing Property Development As a Major Source for Financing Mass Transit Systems

Land should be available at prices that do not reflect speculation on the future development of mass transit systems, so that the full appreciation of land price from a development can be fully captured. The government's role in ensuring this is essential (Boxes 16 and 17).

## Performing Land Value Capture

In cities with private land ownership, taxes are an important tool to recover public investments through LVC (Box 18). Taxes and charges are based on periodically updated official government rates for the market value of land. This enables land-based tools to actually capture appreciation in land value.

## Box 16: Rail+Property Funding: Hong Kong, China; Shenzhen; and Singapore

In Hong Kong, China and Shenzhen, viability gap funding for mass rapid transit projects is usually in the form of land grants by the government. In these cities, the state owns the land and controls the supply via periodic auctions.

In Singapore, though land is not directly used for mass rapid transit financing, it does fuel a large portion of government capital grants. Although property ownership in Singapore was not nationalized by law, the government has acquired large land parcels. From 1960 to 2007, the share of land in Singapore owned by the public sector (including statutory boards) approximately doubled, from 44% to over 85%. Some important features in Singapore's land laws in the past have enabled this, including the provision to acquire land at prices existing at a specific historic date rather than current prices, provisions to discount from the compensation payable recent price increases due to public investment in the area, and a provision that allows the government to acquire land for residential and commercial development in addition to public purposes.

Source: CRISIL

## Box 17: Property Development on Private Land: Taipei,China

In the joint development practiced in Taipei,China, the government does not acquire land. Private landowners are encouraged to participate in a consolidated project, which includes development of the transit station and real estate.

The project is permitted to be developed with larger floor space given the larger plot size and regulatory relaxations available for mass rapid transit projects. The proceeds of the real estate project are required to cover not only the cost of construction, the developer's profits, and the landowner's compensation, but also the cost of constructing the mass rapid transit station.

Joint development schemes, though substantially implemented, do not apply to all transit station developments. The network has more than 130 transit stations, but only 60 have entered into joint development.

Source: CRISIL.

## Box 18: Tax-Based Land Value Capture Sources: Taipei,China

In Taipei,China, most transit stations are developed through private real estate investments under the joint development scheme. The city government bears the costs of the remaining stations and other mass rapid transit infrastructure. Land-based taxes contributed an average of 77.5% of Taipei,China's tax revenue in fiscal years 2018 and 2019.

Three major land-based tax revenue sources are:

- **Land value increment tax.** This is the largest tax source for the city government and constitutes more than 30% of its total revenue. The tax is levied on appreciation of property value and is telescopically set to the extent of the increase from 20% (for appreciation of less than 100%) up to 40% (for price appreciation in excess of 200%).
- **Land value tax.** This is about a quarter of total revenue. It is levied on the relative value of property in comparison to a standard value (starting cumulative value [SVC]), which is the average value of a 7-acre land in the municipality (not considering land used for factories, mining, and agriculture; and tax-exempt land). The tax rate ranges from 1.5% of the property value (property value is 5 times the SCV) to 5.5% (more than 20 times the SCV).
- **House tax.** This constitutes 21.6% of total revenue and is levied on built property. The tax rate is set at 1.2% of the value of residential buildings.

Source: CRISIL.

# Implementing Transit-Oriented Development in India: Observations and Way Forward

TOD is likely to generate multiple benefits in India, especially in terms of sustainability and livability. Its successful implementation calls for strengthening the institutional, planning, and financing frameworks. The qualitative analysis in the previous sections indicates the following:

(i)   Cities in India have created policies to encourage densification and development within transit influence zones but have applied a one-size-fits-all approach by providing higher FAR along the entire length of transit corridors rather than linking the FAR to node and place values.

(ii)  A mechanism for coordinating across various institutions is still a key issue, especially to guide transport planning and its integration with land use planning.

(iii) Land-based revenue such as LVC is a major financing source for mass transit projects, particularly when linked to TOD. However, there is only a limited use of LVC for financing such mass transit projects.

In addition, India exhibits a horizontally expanding spatial form, limited public transport availability, large commuting distances, and increasing use of private transport. Accumulation of private vehicles in the central areas of cities causes congestion, air pollution, and road safety issues that, in the long term, will cause a detrimental impact on urban sustainability, livability, resilience, and even economic potential.

Per international practice, integration between land use and transport planning practices can address critical issues, such as by mitigating urban sprawl, encouraging development within transit influence zones, and enabling own-source revenue from land value. Clearly, improved land use planning and management can support the creation of added value around the TOD system.

To validate this idea, further tests and simulations are required to fill knowledge gaps. The rest of this report explores the impact of one important element of land use planning—FAR regulation—on city-level outcomes in Bengaluru. Specifically, the report carries out simulations to estimate the effect of relaxing the FAR on densification, value of time, property values, and wages around the Bengaluru metro corridor. This allows quantification of the direct and wider economic benefits associated with integrated land use planning and TOD.

# Spatial Analysis of Bengaluru's Transit-Oriented Development and Comparisons with Asian Cities

**4**

The qualitative analysis in the previous chapter indicates that various factors influence the successful implementation of TOD. The experiences across the cities studied suggest that land use management, in particular, is a critical factor that can generate multiple positive socioeconomic externalities in the context of TOD. To grasp the quantitative importance of getting land use policies right, this part of the report carries out simulations to examine how city-level outcomes vary across different scenarios for a particular type of land use regulation: FAR. It does so using the case of Bengaluru.

The analysis is carried out in two steps. This chapter describes the urban form, density regulations, and socioeconomic characteristics of Bengaluru and four Asian cities: Guangzhou, Hyderabad, Seoul, and Shenzhen. A quantitative assessment of how various scenarios for FAR along the Bengaluru metro corridor may impact urban form and economic activity follows in Chapter 5.

## Measuring Upward and Outward Expansion

The analysis of urban form of Bengaluru and four peer cities[4] focuses on outward expansion and densification. Table 16 shows comparative statistics of the five cities.

### Table 16: Size and Station Parameters of Peer Cities

| City | Computed Area (square kilometer) | Population 2015 (million) | Metro Construction Began (year) | Metro First Operational (year) | Metro Stations Analyzed |
|------|------|------|------|------|------|
| Bengaluru | 708 | 10.14 | 2007 | 2011 | 116 |
| Guangzhou | 7,434 | 11.69 | 1993 | 1997 | 311 |
| Hyderabad | 637 | 8.70 | 2012 | 2017 | 59 |
| Seoul | 605 | 10.35 | 1971 | 1974 | 273 |
| Shenzhen | 1,997 | 11.38 | 1998 | 2004 | 258 |

Source: World Resources Institute (WRI) India.

---

4    The four peer cities (Guangzhou, Hyderabad, Seoul, and Shenzhen) were selected based on their having (i) an operational metro network, (ii) similar population size as Bengaluru, and (iii) supportive TOD/density regulations.

The horizontal growth data reveal major changes that occurred in the last few decades (Figures 3–6).

(i)    Comparing the changes in the impervious area at city scale, Seoul had the highest impervious area among the five cities for all years from 1985 to 2015.[5] However, it had the lowest increase in impervious area over time. The impervious areas in Bengaluru and Hyderabad were almost 20 percentage points lower than in Seoul in 1988. Guangzhou and Shenzhen, two cities in the People's Republic of China (PRC), had the lowest impervious areas in 1988. Shenzhen urbanized at a faster rate and experienced more outward or horizontal growth as compared with Guangzhou.

(ii)   Seoul had the highest percentage of impervious area around the metro catchment area among the cities. The Hyderabad metro catchment area had a higher share of impervious area than Bengaluru. This could be because the analysis for Bengaluru included all current and future metro stations and Hyderabad metro was built mostly along the developed parts of the city.

### Figure 3: Percent Impervious Area by Year, City Scale

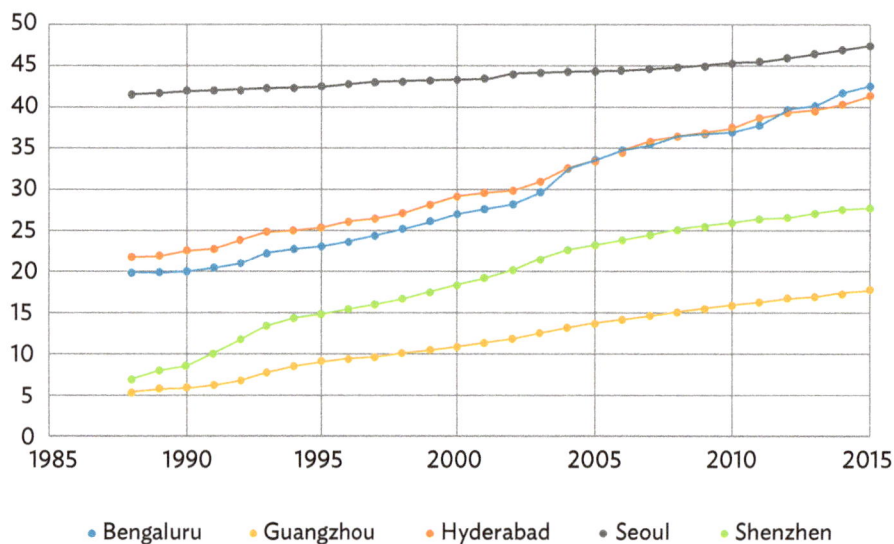

• Bengaluru    • Guangzhou    • Hyderabad    • Seoul    • Shenzhen

Source: World Resources Institute (WRI) India, based on data from World Settlement Footprint (WSF) Imperviousness layer, German Aerospace Center (DLR).

---

[5]    "Impervious area" can be defined as surfaces consisting of materials such as asphalt, concrete, or stone that seal the soil surface, eliminating water infiltration. They are primarily associated with streets, sidewalks, and building structures.

## Figure 4: Percent Impervious Area around Metro Stations by Year, Metro Scale

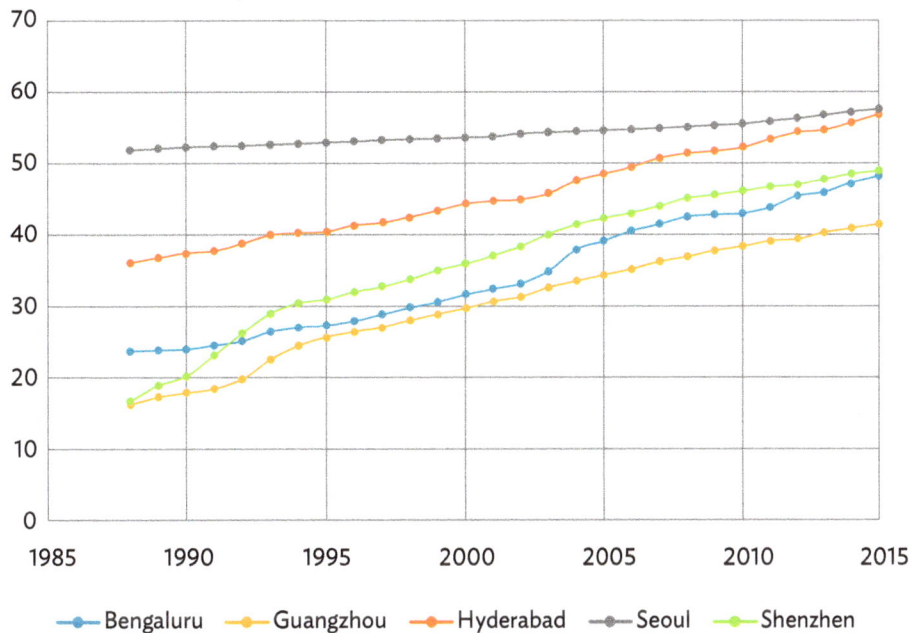

Source: World Resources Institute (WRI) India, based on data from World Settlement Footprint (WSF) Imperviousness layer, German Aerospace Center (DLR).

## Figure 5: Annual Increase in Impervious Area

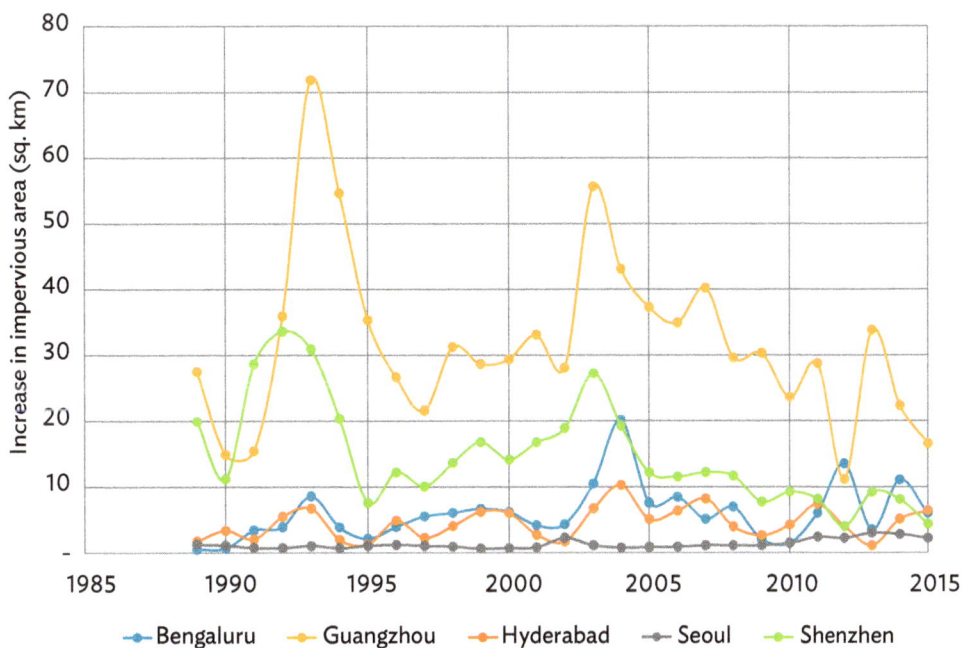

sq. km = square kilometer.
Source: World Resources Institute (WRI) India, based on data from World Settlement Footprint (WSF) Imperviousness layer, German Aerospace Center (DLR).

## Figure 6: Annual Impervious Area Growth Rate

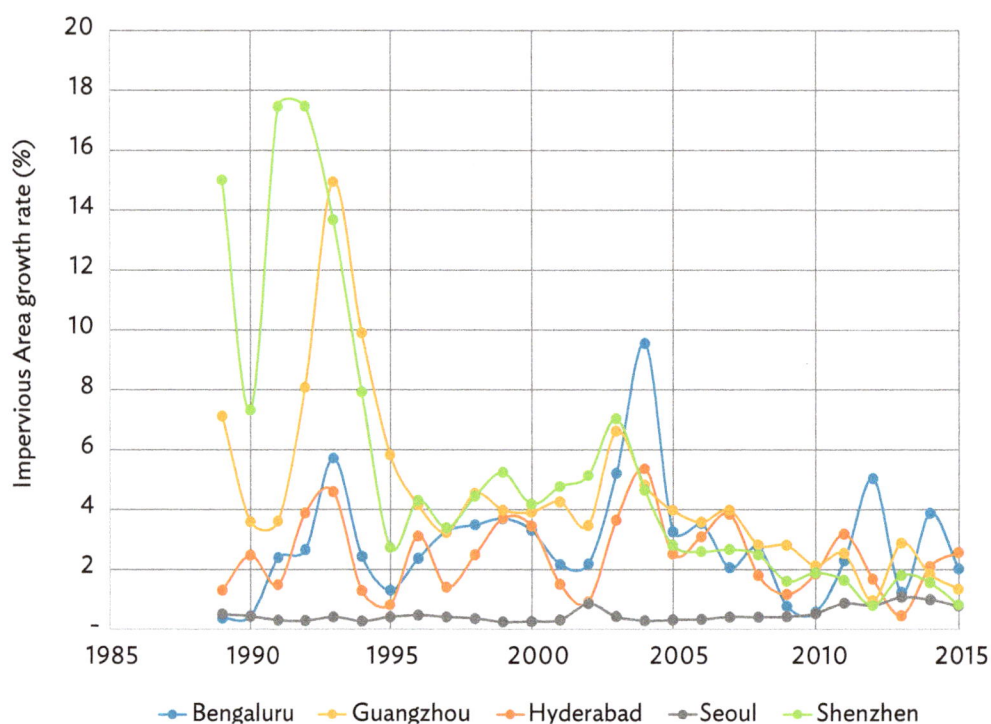

Source: World Resources Institute (WRI) India, based on data from World Settlement Footprint (WSF) Imperviousness layer, German Aerospace Center (DLR).

(iii)   Focusing on the horizonal growth of the five cities between 1988 and 2015, Guangzhou's horizontal or outward growth was more than the combined outward growth of all four cities (Table 17). Bengaluru grew horizontally at 6 square kilometers (km$^2$) annually (1988 and 2015) and on average grew outwardly at the rate of 7.8 km$^2$ annually from 2003 to 2015 and 4.25 km$^2$ annually from 1988 to 2003 (Figure 7).

### Table 17: Magnitude of Horizontal Growth, 1988–2015

| City | Total Impervious Area Added, 1988–2015 (square kilometer) | Annual Average Increase of Impervious Area (square kilometer) |
|------|---|---|
| Bengaluru | 161.52 | 5.98 |
| Guangzhou | 862.00 | 32.00 |
| Hyderabad | 121.60 | 4.50 |
| Seoul | 35.00 | 1.30 |
| Shenzhen | 400.00 | 14.80 |

Source: World Resources Institute (WRI) India, based on World Settlement Footprint (WSF) Evolution Data, German Aerospace Center (DLR).

**Figure 7: Evolution of Urbanization in Bengaluru, 1985–2015**

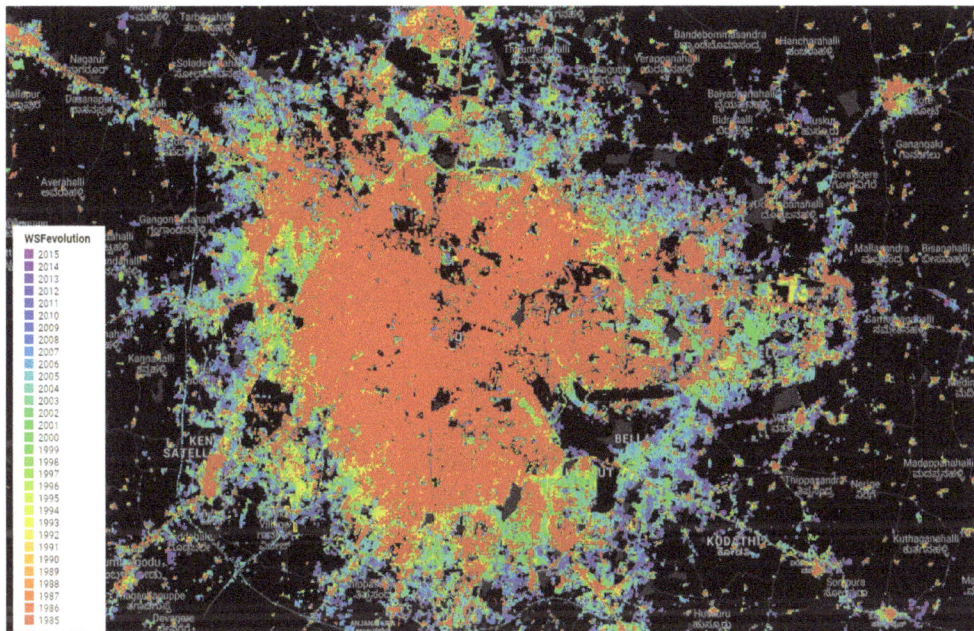

Source: World Resources Institute (WRI) India, based on World Settlement Footprint (WSF) Evolution Data, German Aerospace Center (DLR).

(iv)    In terms of population growth (Figure 8):

- Shenzhen's population grew from 193,000 in 1985 to 12.3 million in 2020. It experienced the fastest population growth, with an annual growth rate of 35% in the late 1980s and a 21% annual growth rate during the 1990s. Guangzhou and Shenzhen experienced similar growth. Guangzhou's population grew from 2.3 million in 1985 to 13.3 million in 2020. Its population had a 6% annual growth rate (AGR) in the late 1980s and a 9% AGR during the entire 1990s. Its growth then dropped to about 2.5% annually and has been constant since then.

- Hyderabad grew at an annual growth rate of 5% in the late 1980s and has experienced a constant annual growth rate of 2.9% from 1985 to 2020. Bengaluru has been growing consistently since 1985. Its AGR was 3.0%–3.5% from 1985 to 2003. The growth rate experienced a slight bump around 2004 and has since been hovering around 4%. The population of Bengaluru increased from 3.4 million in 1985 to 12.0 million in 2019. It also experienced greater outward growth during this time, indicating that the city's vertical growth may not be as high as that of its international peer cities.

- Seoul has a very different experience than the other four cities. It had the highest population between 1985 and 2005. Seoul's population peaked at 10.5 million in 1990 and declined slightly after that until about the year 2000. The population of Seoul is now 9.9 million, like that of Hyderabad.

### Figure 8: Population Trends Comparison, 1985–2015
(million)

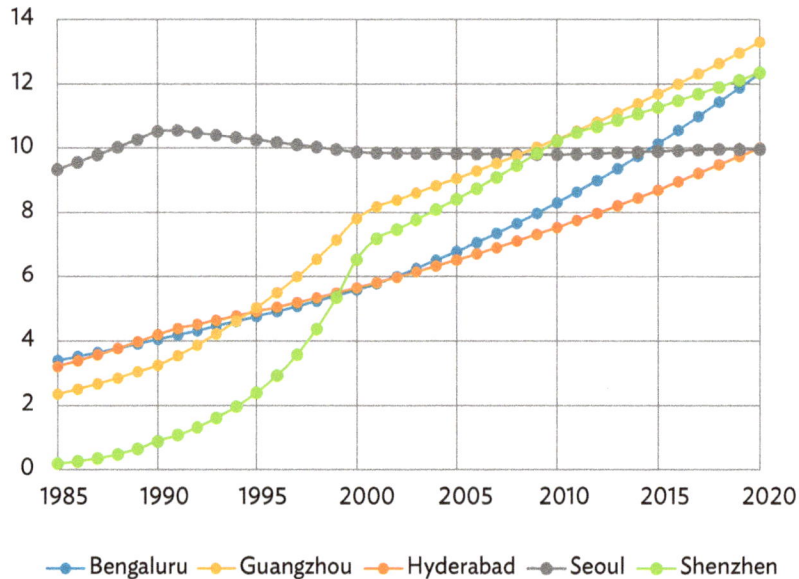

Source: World Resources Institute (WRI) India, based on United Nations Department of Economic and Social Affairs, World Population Prospects, 2019 (https://population.un.org/wpp).

(v)   Finally, all five cities other than Seoul experienced significant outward growth between 1985 and 2005. Guangzhou and Shenzhen, as well as Seoul, then established and implemented urban redevelopment plans and projects to slow this trend. The result was a proliferation of high-rise and high-density buildings (Figures 9 and 10). This is evident from the number of skyscrapers (greater than 150 meters height) that were built in the three cities since the mid-1990s. Bengaluru does not have skyscrapers, but based on data from EMPORIS, construction of buildings taller than 100 meters began around 2007.[6]

An in-depth analysis of 2015 World Settlement Footprint (WSF) 3D 90-meter resolution data was conducted to compare the vertical profile at city and metro scales. Figure 11 provides a snapshot of the vertical profiles at the metro station scale. Several observations emerge from the analysis. First, Guangzhou and Shenzhen have the tallest buildings of the five cities, with significantly more pixels having an average bin height greater than 10 m. Seoul comes next, followed by Bengaluru and then Hyderabad. Second, the two Indian cities have very few pixels that are taller than 10 m than the international peers. This can be attributed to stringent regulations that inhibit consumption of the maximum permissible FAR. Third, of the very few pixels higher than 10 m in Bengaluru, about 95% are within the metro catchment area. These shares are lower in peer cities, indicating that Bengaluru has room for FAR relaxation beyond the metro catchment area.

As remote sensing data from 1985 to 2015 show, Bengaluru and Hyderabad grew more in the outward direction; the two PRC cities, Guangzhou and Shenzhen, grew both outward and upward; and Seoul grew in the upward direction. Vertically, the two Indian cities are shorter than their international counterparts, both around metro stations and across the city in general.

---

[6]   German Aerospace Center (DLR) World Settlement Footprint 3D data, World Resources International. Seoul, Guangzhou, and Shenzhen: Buildings >= 150m height only, hence no buildings <40; Bengaluru: Buildings >=100m, Maximum Height - 123 m Hyderabad: #Floors, No height information was available.

## Figure 9: Timeline for Development of Skyscrapers

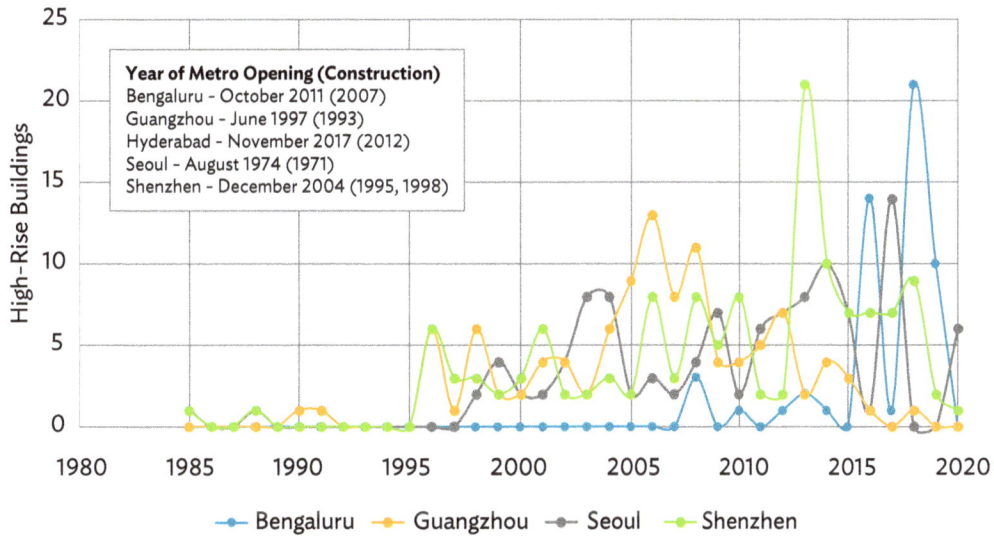

**Year of Metro Opening (Construction)**
Bengaluru - October 2011 (2007)
Guangzhou - June 1997 (1993)
Hyderabad - November 2017 (2012)
Seoul - August 1974 (1971)
Shenzhen - December 2004 (1995, 1998)

Source: World Resources Institute (WRI) India, based on EMPORIS dataset (https://www.emporis.com).

## Figure 10: Number of Buildings by Building Height Range

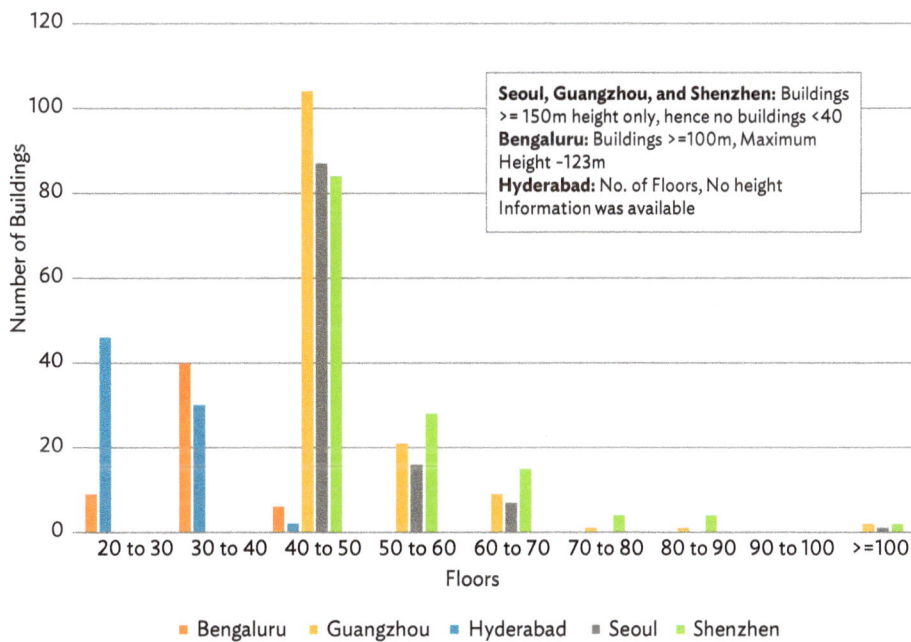

**Seoul, Guangzhou, and Shenzhen:** Buildings >= 150m height only, hence no buildings <40
**Bengaluru:** Buildings >=100m, Maximum Height ~123m
**Hyderabad:** No. of Floors, No height Information was available

m = meter.

Notes: The figure shows the number of high-rises in each city in terms of number of floors. Data includes buildings greater than 150 meters height for Seoul, Guangzhou, and Shenzhen, and buildings greater than 100 meters for Bengaluru. For Hyderabad, the data includes number of floors directly instead of height information.

Source: World Resources Institute (WRI) India, based on EMPORIS dataset (https://www.emporis.com).

## Figure 11: Frequency Distribution Comparison of Pixels by Height Bins around Metro Stations

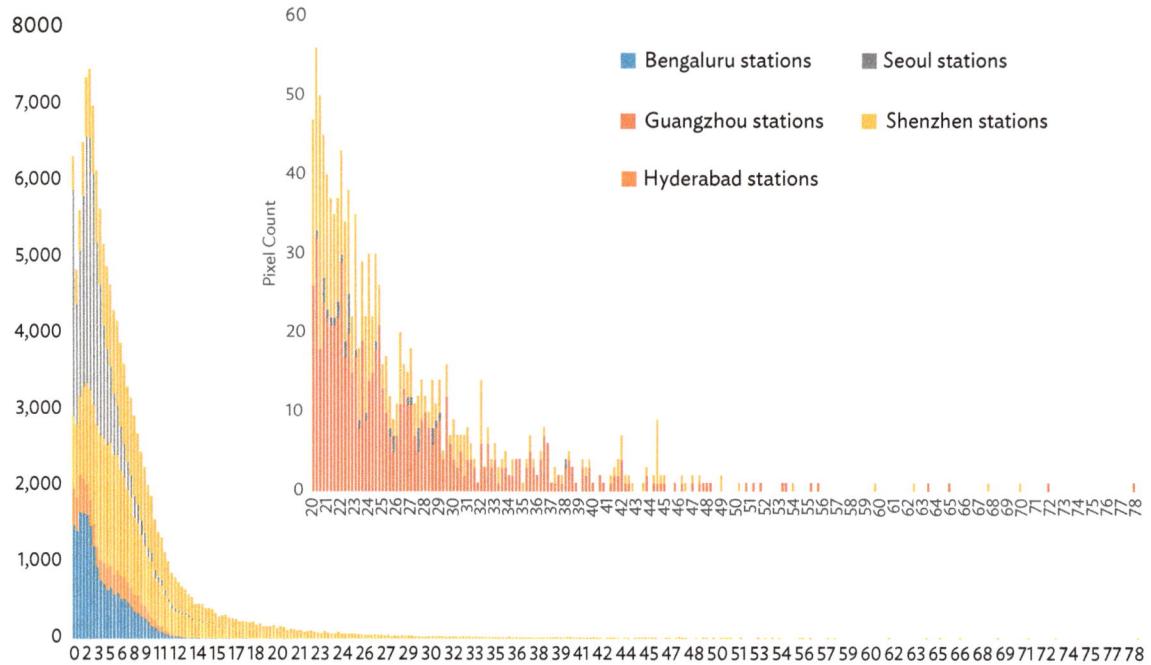

Source: World Resources Institute (WRI) India, based on DLR World Settlement Footprint (WSF) 3D Data, German Aerospace Center (DLR).

# Exploring Built Form and Job Distribution

The analysis so far has shown that Bengaluru grew outward more than upward. Current land use regulations are likely to have supported such a pattern. This section focuses on the urban form and spatial distribution of population and employment inside the Bruhat Bengaluru Mahanagara Palika (BBMP) boundary. The analysis aims to help understand the socioeconomic dynamics related to the metro network in Bengaluru and to set the baseline scenario for the later simulations on densification.

Based on data from the 2011 census, Rail India Technical and Economic Service Limited (RITES) 2015 travel survey, 2018–2019 Annual Survey of Industries Frame, and planned and existing metro station locations, the analysis reveals that:

(i)     The 198 wards in the BBMP boundary had a total population of approximately 9.5 million and had 4.12 million jobs in 2015. Slum dwellers made up 7.9% of the total population. The average workforce participation rate of the BBMP was 48.3%.

(ii)    Of the 198 wards, 72% (143) have varying levels (0.1%–100.0% of the ward area) of access to the current and future phases of Bengaluru Metro Rail Corporation Limited stations.[7]

---

[7]    "Metro access area" is defined as within a 1 km Euclidian radius of a metro station. All the current and future metro stations were used for this analysis.

(iii) Approximately 43% of the population living within the BBMP boundary will have access to the metro once all the phases are built.

(iv) Of all the jobs inside the BBMP boundary, 50% will be accessible to metro riders; 43% of the people in the labor force, and 42% of the slum population will also have access to the metro.

(v) Based on the sector distribution of jobs reported in the 2018–2019 Annual Survey of Industries Frame, metro riders will have access to 44% of manufacturing-related jobs. A similar analysis of the white-collar jobs data indicates that 55% of them will be accessible to metro riders when all phases are built.

To understand the population and employment spread around the city, all the above attributes were also studied based on their relation to the Outer Ring Road (ORR). Following this, the data reveal that:

(i) Of the 198 wards, 132 (66.7%) are inside the ORR, and this study refers to them as "the core city."

(ii) About 56.7% of the population (5.4 million), 63.1% of jobs (2.6 million), and 64.5% of slum dwellers (484,000) are inside the ORR. Of the workforce, 56.1% (2.3 million) live inside the ORR.

(iii) The core city has only 30% of the total BBMP land area, but almost twice the share of the population and more than twice the share of employment. This makes the core city very dense in terms of population and employment. The core city has a population density of 34,568 persons per km$^2$ and is 2.6 times denser than the area outside the ORR. Similarly, its employment density of 17,166 jobs per km$^2$ is 3 times greater than that outside ORR. The above findings can be observed clearly in Figures 12 and 13.

(iv) While 19 of the top 20 populated wards are outside the ORR, 100% of the top 20 densest populated wards are in the core city. The core city has 70% of the top 20 employment wards and 85% of the top densest employment wards.

(v) Of the 5.4 million people residing inside the ORR, 2.8 million (52%) live within a 1 km radius of a metro station. Inside the ORR, 58.1% of the jobs, 50.1% of the workforce, and 47.5% of slum dwellers are within 1 km of at least one metro station.

(vi) The spatial distribution of jobs by sector shows that 73% of manufacturing jobs are in the wards outside the core city, while 63% of white-collar jobs are in the core city and only 37% are outside the ORR.

## Figure 12: Population and Population Density Distribution, 2015

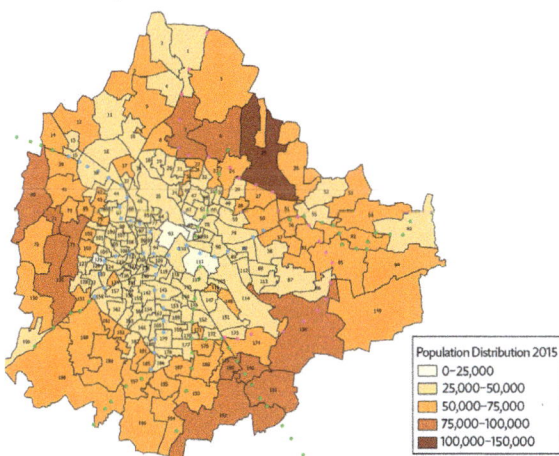

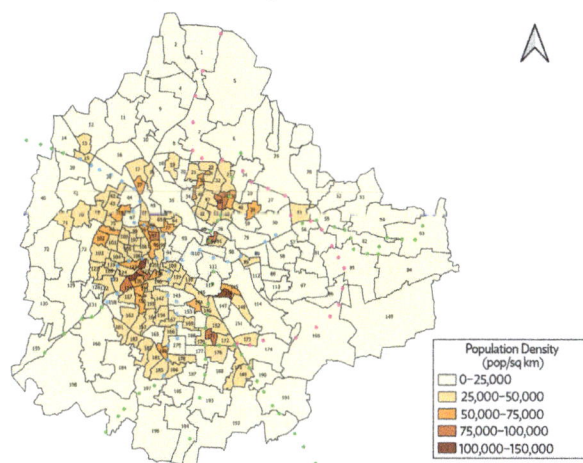

BBMP = Bruhat Bengaluru Mahanagara Palika.
Source: World Resources Institute (WRI) India, based on data from Rail India Technical and Economic Service Limited (RITES) Feasibility Report, 2015.

## Figure 13: Employment and Employment Density Distribution Maps

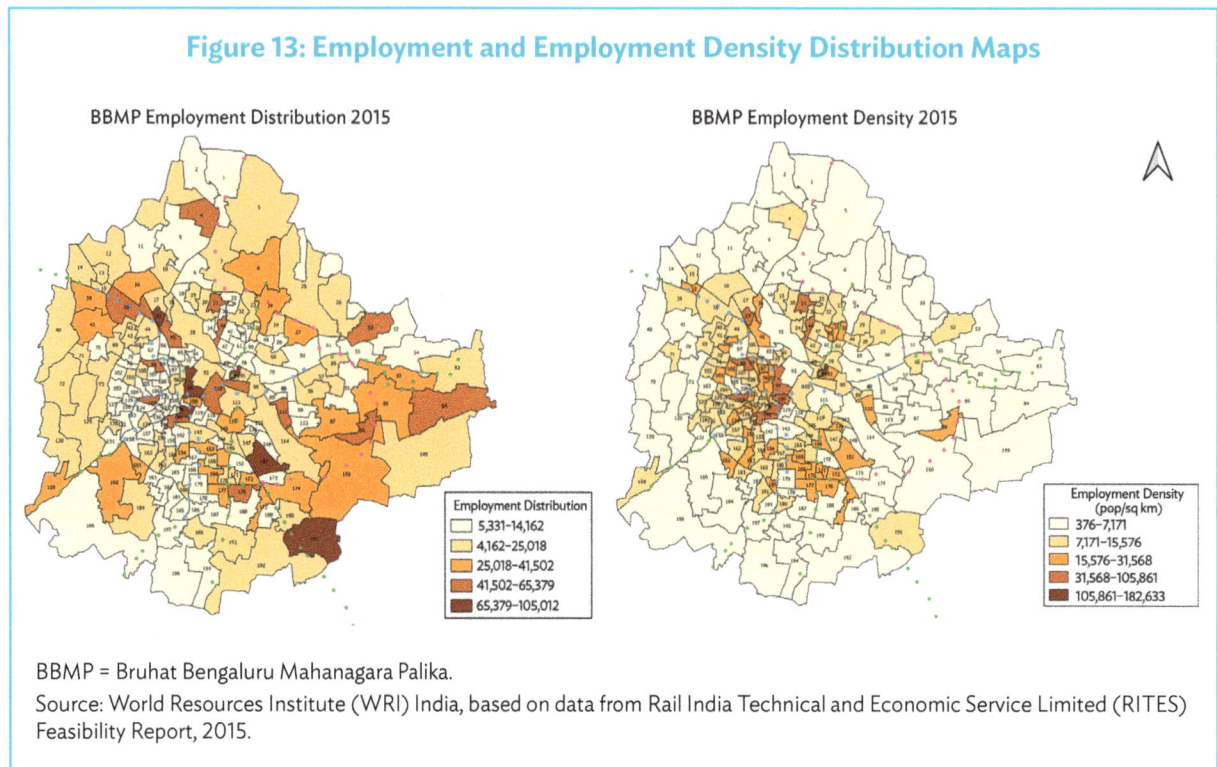

BBMP Employment Distribution 2015

BBMP Employment Density 2015

Employment Distribution
- 5,331–14,162
- 4,162–25,018
- 25,018–41,502
- 41,502–65,379
- 65,379–105,012

Employment Density
(pop/sq km)
- 376–7,171
- 7,171–15,576
- 15,576–31,568
- 31,568–105,861
- 105,861–182,633

BBMP = Bruhat Bengaluru Mahanagara Palika.
Source: World Resources Institute (WRI) India, based on data from Rail India Technical and Economic Service Limited (RITES)
Feasibility Report, 2015.

The proportion of jobs available to the total workforce was estimated for each of the 198 wards[8] as the ratio of jobs available to the workforce participation rate. The wards shown in dark red color are in the center of the city and have the highest jobs available/workforce participation values, ranging from 5 to 8. This means that these wards have 5–8 times more jobs than the number of workers living there: 135 (68%) of the 198 wards had a value greater than 1. These wards should be considered as "trip attractors" given the many commuters who travel to them for work from their wards of residence (Figure 14). The other 63 wards are "trip generators" from which commuters travel outside for work.

Many factors in addition to location of work, determine where people choose to live, including cost of living, proximity of good schools, proximity of a working spouse's work, accessibility to amenities, and commuting time. A close examination of the ward and workplace location data from the Household Travel Survey of 2015 confirms the preceding hypothesis. Specifically, 190 (96%) of the 198 wards have more working individuals traveling outside the ward for work than working in the ward.

---

[8]    A value of less than 1 indicates that there are fewer jobs in the ward than the workforce living inside it. Similarly, if the value is greater than 1, the ward has more jobs than the workforce residing there.

**Figure 14: Jobs Available versus Workforce Participation, by Ward**

BBMP Jobs Available to Workforce Participation, 2015

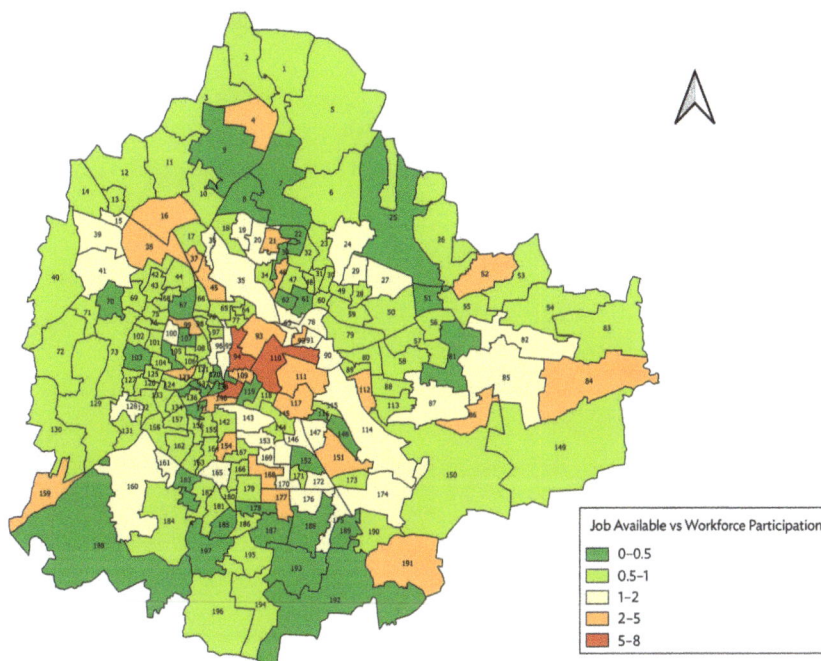

Job Available vs Workforce Participation
- 0–0.5
- 0.5–1
- 1–2
- 2–5
- 5–8

BBMP = Bruhat Bengaluru Mahanagara Palika.
Source: World Resources Institute (WRI) India, based on data from Rail India Technical and Economic Service Limited (RITES) Feasibility Report, 2015.

# Socioeconomic Characteristics and Travel Patterns

The socioeconomic characteristics of households in Bengaluru complete this descriptive analysis. The following notable findings were gleaned from the analysis of the 2015 RITES travel survey data:

(i)    A majority of households (75%) comprised three to four persons. Households with five to six people constituted the second highest group (16%). The average household size was 3.7.

(ii)   About 60% of households had "two-wheelers," 20% had cars, and 16% had no vehicles.[9] Of the people who owned cars, 95.5% had one car in the household.

(iii)  About 21% of households had monthly incomes less than or equal to rupees (₹)15,000 ($204)[10] and another 28% earned ₹15,001–₹25,000 per month. The share of households with monthly income more than ₹25,000 was 51%. The average household income per month in the study area was ₹32,374.

(iv)   About 21% of households spent ₹1,000 or less per month on transport and nearly 42% spent ₹1,501–₹2,500 monthly on transport. Over 37% of households spent more than ₹2,500 per month on transport. Average expenditure on transport per household is estimated at ₹2,473 per month, which is 7.6% of the average household income.

(v)    In terms of education attainment, graduates and post-graduate individuals accounted for nearly 36%.

---

9    The term "two-wheelers" refers mostly to two-wheel motorized vehicles (motorcycles, scooters, mopeds, etc.).
10   The Indian rupee–United States dollar exchange rate used throughout this document is 73.53:1 (i.e., that in December 2019).

The characteristics of work and home locations of the individuals earning high and low wages are investigated in detail.[11] The following are some of the observations:

(i)     Three-quarters of the top 20 wards with the highest number of jobs were also in the list of top 20 wards where the highest-income and lowest-income earning individuals worked. Thus, the majority of the top employment wards have both high- and low-end jobs.

(ii)    Of the top 20 wards where individuals earning low incomes worked, only three coincided with the top 20 home location wards of such individuals. The same was true for high-quality or Highest-Income-Earning jobs. Thus, most of the people in both categories do not live in the same ward where they work, and are likely to travel outside their ward for work.

(iii)   Most (85%) of the top 20 wards where low-income earning individuals live are outside the ORR. And most (70%) of the top 20 home location wards of the lowest-income earners will have varying levels (1.2% to 90.0%) of access to the metro. About 40% of these will have at least 25% of the ward area that is accessible when all phases of the metro are operating.

(iv)    Over half (60%) of the top 20 home location wards of the highest-income earning individuals are outside the ORR, and 85% of the 20 wards will have varying levels of access (1.8% to 92.6%) to the metro.

## Figure 15: Top Residential Wards of Lowest- and Highest-Income Earning Groups

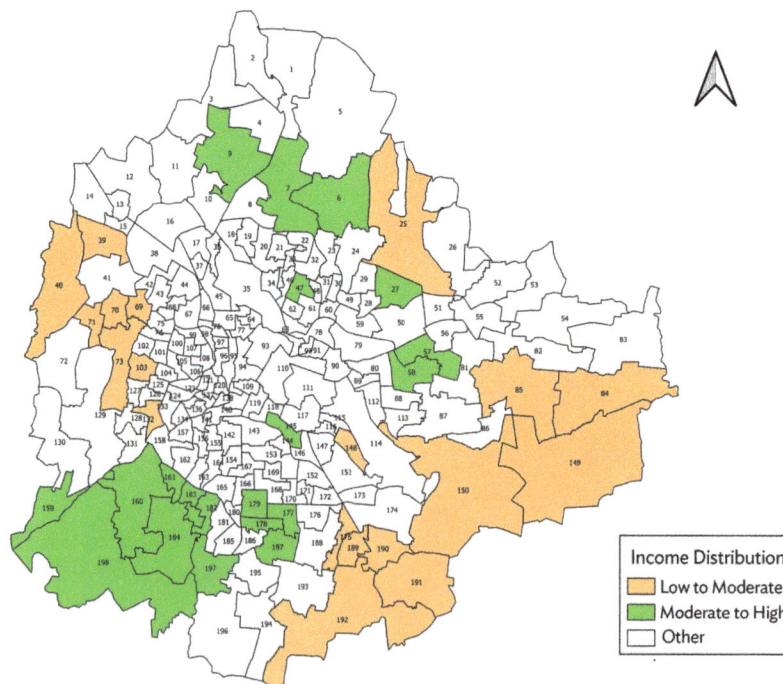

Source: World Resources Institute (WRI) India, based on data from Rail India Technical and Economic Service Limited (RITES) Feasibility Report, 2015.

---

[11]    Individual monthly salary that was captured as part of the Household Travel Survey was categorized as low (<₹18,200), moderate (>₹18,200 and <₹31,800), medium (>₹31,800 and <₹85,600), and high (>₹85,600). For simplicity, low and moderate groups were combined as the lowest income, and medium and high groups were combined as the highest income categories.

Figure 15 shows the residential wards of the top 20 highest- and lowest-income-earning groups. Eighty-five percent of the top 20 low-to-moderate income wards and 60% of the medium-to-high income wards are outside the ORR. A majority of the top 20 low-income wards are in the southeast and west sides of the ORR. A majority of the top 20 high-income wards are in the southwest of the ORR.

On the other hand, the evaluation of work-related trips by travel mode and distance to work of the top 20 residential wards of the lowest- and highest-income-earning individuals (Tables 18 and 19), demonstrates that:

(i)     In the wards where the lowest-income earners lived, the majority commuted to work on a two-wheeler (41.5%) or by bus (29.2%).

(ii)    In the wards where the highest-income earners lived, the majority commuted by car (39.2%) or a two-wheeler (35.3%).

(iii)   The lowest-income earners tend to travel shorter distances across all modes.

### Table 18: Transport Mode Choice of Top 20 Residential Wards by Income Group (%)

| Travel Mode Share (km) | Top 20 Residential Wards of | |
|---|---|---|
| | Lowest-Income Earners | Highest-Income Earners |
| Car | 13.9 | 39.2 |
| Two-wheeler[a] | 41.5 | 35.3 |
| Bus | 29.2 | 20.3 |
| Walk | 8.1 | 1.1 |

[a]  The term "two-wheelers" refers mostly to two-wheel motorized vehicles (motorcycles, scooters, mopeds, etc.).
Source: World Resources Institute (WRI) India, based on data from Rail India Technical and Economic Service Limited (RITES) Feasibility Report, 2015.

### Table 19: Average Distance to Work by Mode for Top 20 Wards by Income Group (km)

| Average Distance to Work | Top 20 Residential Wards of | |
|---|---|---|
| | Lowest-Income Earners | Highest-Income Earners |
| Car | 11.1 | 14.0 |
| Two-wheeler[a] | 8.0 | 9.6 |
| Bus | 9.6 | 16.3 |
| Walk | 1.0 | 0.5 |

km = kilometer.
[a]  The term "two-wheelers" refers mostly to two-wheel motorized vehicles (motorcycles, scooters, mopeds, etc.).
Source: World Resources Institute (WRI) India, based on data from Rail India Technical and Economic Service Limited (RITES) Feasibility Report, 2015.

These results are confirmed by the individual-level travel characteristics analysis from the travel survey.

(i)     About 26% of the daily trips were made by walking; 27% by two-wheelers ; and 32% by public transport modes, including bus, minibus, school bus, chartered bus, and metro (Table 20). The average number of trips (including by walking) was 1.24; excluding walking, it was 0.92, and for motorized trips it was 0.91.

(ii)   Of the total motorized trips in Bengaluru, 44% traveled using public transit and 37% of the commuters used two-wheelers.

(iii)  Eighty percent of the daily trips were for work and education, and 20% were for shopping, social, medical, and recreation purposes.

(iv)   The average length of trips made by walking was 2.0 km, by two-wheeler was 8.1 km, by car was 12.2 km, by taxi was 12.7 km, and by bus was 9.7 km.

(v)    The average travel time for one-way work trips outside the ward was 52 minutes.

Figure 16 compares the same information across five major modes of transport for work-related trips. Individuals earning low incomes predominantly prefer to use two-wheelers and public transport (bus), while individuals earning high incomes used cars.

## Table 20: Work Trip Mode Shares by Income Level
### (%)

| Commute Mode Shares | Low-Income Individuals | Moderate-Income Individuals | Medium-Income Individuals | High-Income Individuals |
|---|---|---|---|---|
| Car | 5.55 | 13.64 | 34.49 | 63.46 |
| Taxi | 0.08 | 0.24 | 0.18 | 0.00 |
| Shared taxi or auto | 0.11 | 0.19 | 0.91 | 1.92 |
| Two-wheeler[a] | 41.65 | 41.83 | 37.39 | 26.92 |
| Auto | 5.74 | 1.40 | 0.77 | 1.92 |
| Bus | 39.79 | 40.27 | 24.21 | 5.77 |
| Minibus | 0.02 | 0.04 | 0.05 | 0.00 |
| School bus | 0.00 | 0.02 | 0.00 | 0.00 |
| Chartered bus | 0.14 | 0.25 | 0.50 | 0.00 |
| Bicycle | 0.71 | 0.19 | 0.05 | 0.00 |
| Train | 0.01 | 0.00 | 0.14 | 0.00 |
| Walk | 6.18 | 1.95 | 1.34 | 0.00 |
| Total | 100.00 | 100.00 | 100.00 | 100.00 |

[a]  The term "two-wheelers" refers mostly to two-wheel motorized vehicles (motorcycles, scooters, mopeds, etc.).
Source: World Resources Institute (WRI) India, based on data from Rail India Technical and Economic Service Limited (RITES) Feasibility Report, 2015.

Figure 17 summarizes the average distance of work-related trips by income level. The average distance for the lowest-income-earning individuals was about 7.7 km versus about 25 km for the highest-income-earning individuals. It can be inferred that the choice of home location of high-income earners is not constrained by where they worked. High-income individuals tend to travel longer distances using their personal cars and two-wheelers whereas low-income individuals tend to stay closer to their work and generally travel shorter distances.

## Figure 16: Work Trip Mode Shares by Income Level
### (%)

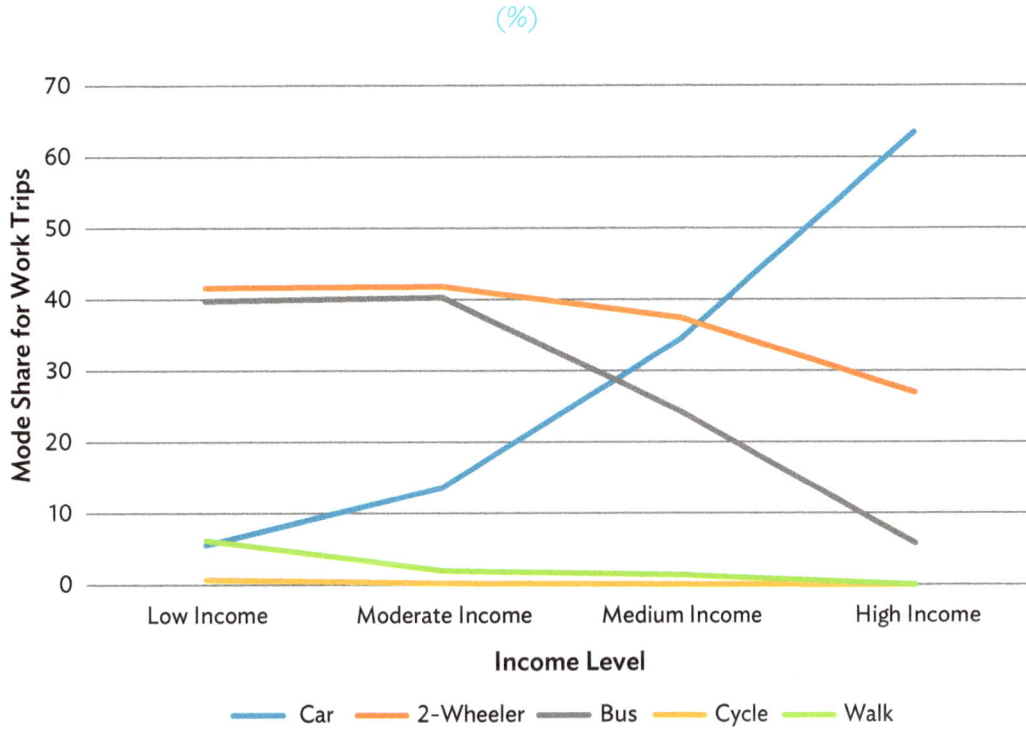

Source: World Resources Institute (WRI) India, based on data from Rail India Technical and Economic Service Limited (RITES) Feasibility Report, 2015.

## Figure 17: Average Distance to Work by Income Level

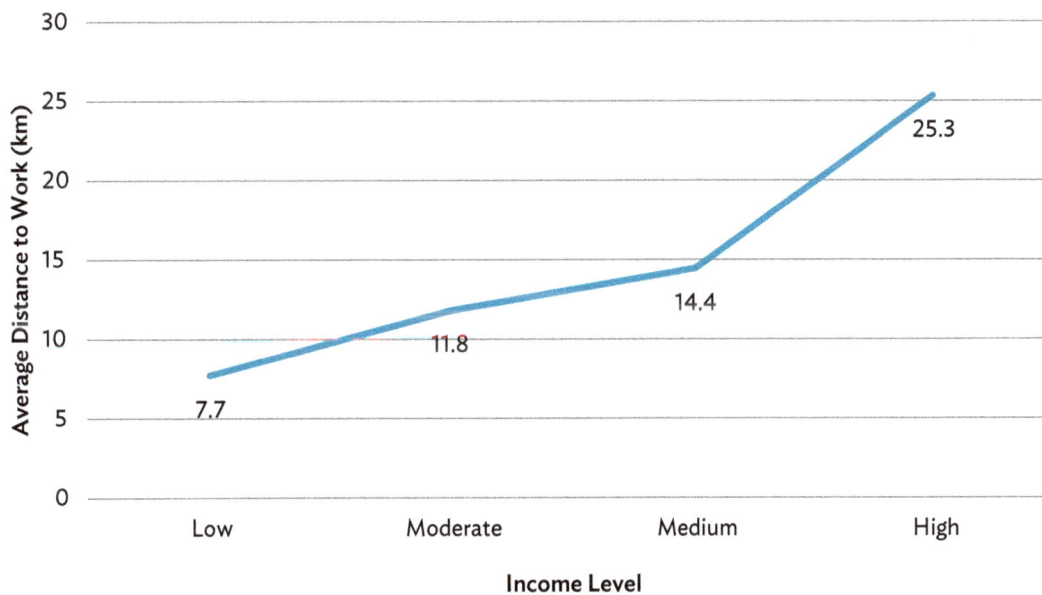

km = kilometer.

Source: World Resources Institute (WRI) India, based on data from Rail India Technical and Economic Service Limited (RITES) Feasibility Report, 2015.

# A Simple Simulation Exercise on How Land Use Policies Affect the Benefits of Transit-Oriented Development

This chapter shows the results from an *ex-ante* analysis of how urban form and socioeconomic benefits from TOD may be impacted by Bengaluru Metro under different configurations for FAR regulations, a key element of land use policies. Specifically, the analysis first considers the densification effect of relaxing FAR regulations in Bengaluru up to the FAR in international cities (regulatory or consumed FAR depending on data availability).[12] Subsequently, based on a cost–benefit framework, the analysis quantifies the effects of the Bengaluru metro network on metro ridership, travel time, property values, property taxes, net profits, and reduction in greenhouse gas emissions of under different FAR scenarios.

The objective of the analysis is not to generate hard predictions, but instead to provide a quantitative sense of how city-level outcomes of interest to policy makers vary under alternative scenarios. The scenarios considered here are chosen to showcase the underlying mechanisms through which transport and urban planning interact. An assumption underlying all the scenarios is that planning, institutional, and financial frameworks function as per best practice.

It must be emphasized that the analysis of how changes in FAR affect city-level outcomes is based on a number of steps and assumptions.

- First, the increase in Bengaluru's FAR across scenarios needs to be determined. Three sets of increases are considered: "aggressive" and "intermediate" increases based on the official regulatory FAR, and actual consumed FAR as detected by remote sensing technology.
- Second, the FAR increases need to be translated into increases in residential and nonresidential floor space.
- Third, the increases in residential floor space are assumed to attract residents to the city and expand the total population of the city proportionally. This is the so-called "open city" assumption with a perfectly elastic supply of migrants utilized by the urban economics literature. The combined effect of increases in both city population and nonresidential floor space translates into increased metro ridership and job density. This assumes that the travel behavior of migrants is the same as that of existing residents and that there are no issues with "first mile and last mile" (FMLM) connectivity when traveling by metro.
- Fourth, the increased metro ridership and job density translate into economic gains for the metro network. The increased metro ridership results in enhanced travel time savings and greenhouse gas emission reduction benefits. Further, adopting values for the elasticity between wage and job density from the

---

[12] In some cases, the maximum permissible FAR based on regulatory framework may not be completely consumed by a city. Hence, ward-level simulated FARs representative of consumed FARs in international cities were also estimated. For further information, see the Appendix.

urban economics literature, the increase in job density gives rise to agglomeration benefits—increases in productivity and/or wages that result when workers and firms interact in close proximity.[13]

- Lastly, the additional floor space results in increase in property value and property tax. This calculation takes into account different unit prices for residential and nonresidential floor space and higher unit construction cost for high-rises and assumes perfectly elastic floor space demand. The Appendix describes several of the key steps and assumptions in detail.

# Additional Floor Space and Gain in Agglomeration Economies

An increase in the FAR will result in increases of residential and nonresidential floor space within the affected wards. For regulatory FAR scenarios, an intermediate FAR increase is applied in each ward if more than 25% of the ward's area is within a 1 km radius of a metro station; and an aggressive FAR increase is applied if any of the ward's area is within a 1 km radius of a metro station. The extent of FAR increase also depends on whether a ward is inside or outside the ORR. For details on FAR increase, see the Appendix. The analysis shows that 60% and 94% of the 198 BBMP wards experience an increase in average FAR for intermediate and aggressive scenarios. Tables 21 and 22 summarize the total additional residential and nonresidential floor space, and additional population that can be accommodated in all 198 wards.

### Table 21: Land Use and Population Changes, Intermediate Scenario

| Scenario | Bengaluru Regulatory FAR | Hyderabad Regulatory FAR | Seoul Regulatory FAR |
|---|---|---|---|
| New average FAR | 2.08 | 2.13 | 2.38 |
| FAR increase | 9.50% | 12.30% | 25.10% |
| Additional floor area, residential (m²) | 28,266,910 | 36,161,359 | 72,165,371 |
| Additional floor area, nonresidential (m²) | 16,095,399 | 21,908,487 | 46,201,521 |
| Additional population | 893,911 | 1,143,564 | 2,282,153 |
| Additional population (share) | 9.40% | 12.10% | 24.10% |

FAR = floor area ratio, m² = square meter.
Source: World Resources Institute (WRI) India, based on World Settlement Footprint (WSF) 3Dimensional (DLR 90m vertical density) and WSF Impervious data, German Aerospace Center (DLR).

### Table 22: Land Use and Population Changes, Aggressive Scenario

| Scenario | Bengaluru regulatory FAR | Hyderabad regulatory FAR | Seoul regulatory FAR |
|---|---|---|---|
| New average FAR | 2.19 | 2.27 | 2.65 |
| FAR increase | 15.3% | 19.6% | 39.5% |
| Additional floor area, residential (m²) | 51,590,726 | 64,780,014 | 126,593,367 |
| Additional floor area, nonresidential (m²) | 25,540,892 | 34,125,255 | 70,765,167 |
| Additional population | 1,631,502 | 2,048,599 | 4,003,380 |
| Additional population (share) | 17.2% | 21.7% | 42.3% |

FAR = floor area ratio, m² = square meter.
Source: World Resources Institute (WRI) India, based on World Settlement Footprint (WSF) 3-Dimensional (DLR 90 m vertical density) and WSF Impervious data, German Aerospace Center (DLR).

---

[13]  Agglomeration benefits arise as workers and firms interact in close physical proximity. Theory suggests that productivity—a fundamental driver of wages—is higher in larger, denser cities because workers are more likely to find jobs that are a good fit, ideas and knowledge are exchanged among individuals and organizations, and resources, including infrastructure, are more easily shared.  See *Asian Development Outlook 2019 Update* for a discussion of agglomeration benefits in the context of developing Asia.

The results presented in the tables show a wide range of density increases that could be realized from various FAR relaxations. The population shifts resulting from the simulations can be understood or visualized in two ways (Figures 18 and 19). The visualizations were developed based on the results for the Seoul FAR simulation based on the intermediate scenario.

## Figure 18: Urban Form Changes under Open City Assumption, Intermediate Scenario

BBMP Population Distribution 2015

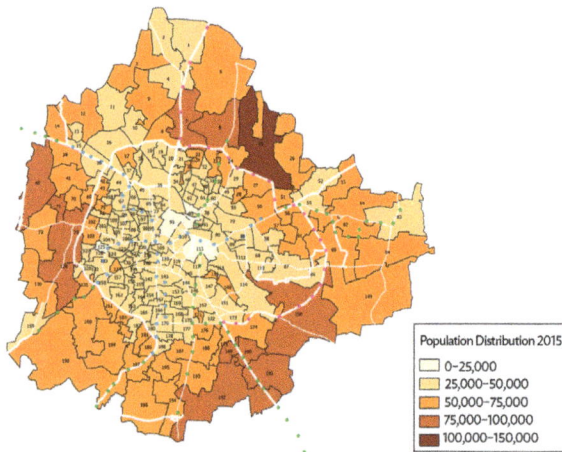

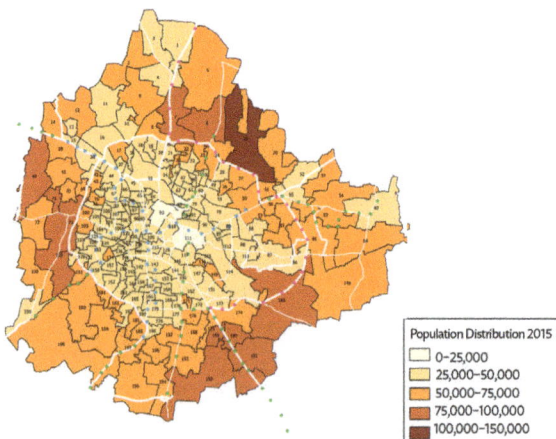

BBMP Population Distribution Shift 2015
ADB Ideal Bangalore Far Simulation 2

Population Distribution 2015
- 0–25,000
- 25,000–50,000
- 50,000–75,000
- 75,000–100,000
- 100,000–150,000

Population Blr Sim2
- 0–25,000
- 25,000–50,000
- 50,000–75,000
- 75,000–100,000
- 100,000–160,000

ADB = Asian Development Bank, BBMP = Bruhat Bengaluru Mahanagara Palika, FAR = floor area ratio.

Source: World Resources Institute (WRI) India, based on data from Rail India Technical and Economic Service Limited (RITES) Feasibility Report, 2015.

## Figure 19: Urban Form Changes under Closed City Assumption, Intermediate Scenario

BBMP Population Distribution 2015

BBMP Controlled Population Distribution Shift 2015
ADB Ideal Seoul FAR Simulation 2

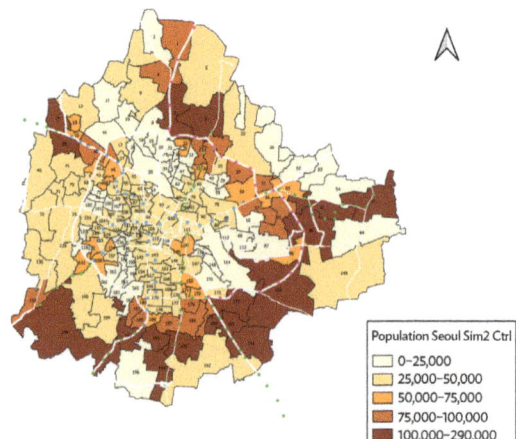

Population Distribution 2015
- 0–25,000
- 25,000–50,000
- 50,000–75,000
- 75,000–100,000
- 100,000–150,000

Population Seoul Sim2 Ctrl
- 0–25,000
- 25,000–50,000
- 50,000–75,000
- 75,000–100,000
- 100,000–290,000

ADB = Asian Development Bank, BBMP = Bruhat Bengaluru Mahanagara Palika, FAR = floor area ratio.

Source: World Resources Institute (WRI) India, based on data from Rail India Technical and Economic Service Limited (RITES) Feasibility Report, 2015.

Under the so-called open city assumption, the additional floor space attracts migrants, and the total population in the city as a whole increases. As seen in the right panel of Figure 18, wards with metro station access experience population increases. Comparing the left-side map with the right-side map, wards that go from a lighter to a darker shade are those with greater increases in population. Most of such changes are observed in wards outside the ORR. Only a handful of wards inside the ORR shift from lighter to darker shades. In contrast, the populations in wards without a metro impact remain the same.

Under the alternative "closed city" assumption, the total BBMP population is kept constant and the net increase in population in affected wards due to simulated increases in the FAR was proportionately offset in unaffected wards. This resulted in population shifts from the unaffected to the affected wards. The color of the wards in Figure 19 that had a decrease in population shifted from darker to lighter shades, while the opposite effect is observed in wards with increased population.

In the following analysis of economic gains, only the "open city" assumption is adopted.

## Travel Time Savings and Environmental Impact

About 96% of the surveyed households in the RITES data indicated that they were willing to shift to public transport if that led to travel time savings of up to 30 minutes. Based on this, the increase in population and commercial space resulting from FAR increases and the availability of the metro are assumed to translate into increased metro ridership (Table 23). The main benefits are shown in Table 24, which reports the monetized value of time savings and carbon dioxide reduction across the scenarios.

### Table 23: Potential Mode Shift to Public Transport

| Time Saved | Respondent Households (#) | Percent |
|---|---|---|
| Up to 10 min | 3,835 | 39.92 |
| Up to 10–20 min | 3,892 | 40.51 |
| Up to 20–30 min | 1,525 | 15.87 |
| Unwilling to shift | 355 | 3.70 |
| Total | 9,607 | 100.00 |

min = minute.
Source: World Resources Institute (WRI) India, based on data from Rail India Technical and Economic Service Limited (RITES) Feasibility Report, 2015.

### Table 24: Comparison of Metro Impact Benefits

| Scenario | Seoul Intermediate Regulatory FAR | Seoul Aggressive Regulatory FAR | Shenzhen Consumed FAR |
|---|---|---|---|
| **Annual time savings** (million hours) | 77 | 93 | 63 |
| **Annual value of time savings** (2020 ₹ million) | 10,002 | 11,927 | 8,008 |
| **Annual GHG Reduction** (tons) | 25,894 | 33,275 | 8,470 |

₹ = rupees, FAR = floor area ratio, GHG = greenhouse gas.
Source: World Resources Institute (WRI) India.

The estimated benefits are sensitive to the time required for FMLM connectivity when traveling in the metro. Based on a survey conducted by the World Resources Institute (WRI) at two metro stations in Bengaluru, metro users spend an average of 30–50 minutes combined for FMLM connectivity. To see how much of the estimate benefit in Table 24 can be realized with or without good accessibility to last mile connectivity, the preceding steps for estimating benefits were repeated for various iterations of travel time required for FMLM.

The analysis shows that the benefits from travel time savings, value of time, and reduction in greenhouse gas emissions are sensitive to the increases in FMLM travel times (Figures 20–22). It is therefore critical to ensure efficient FMLM connectivity at the metro stations to maximize the benefits.

**Figure 20: Travel Time Savings Sensitivity to First Mile and Last Mile Travel Times**

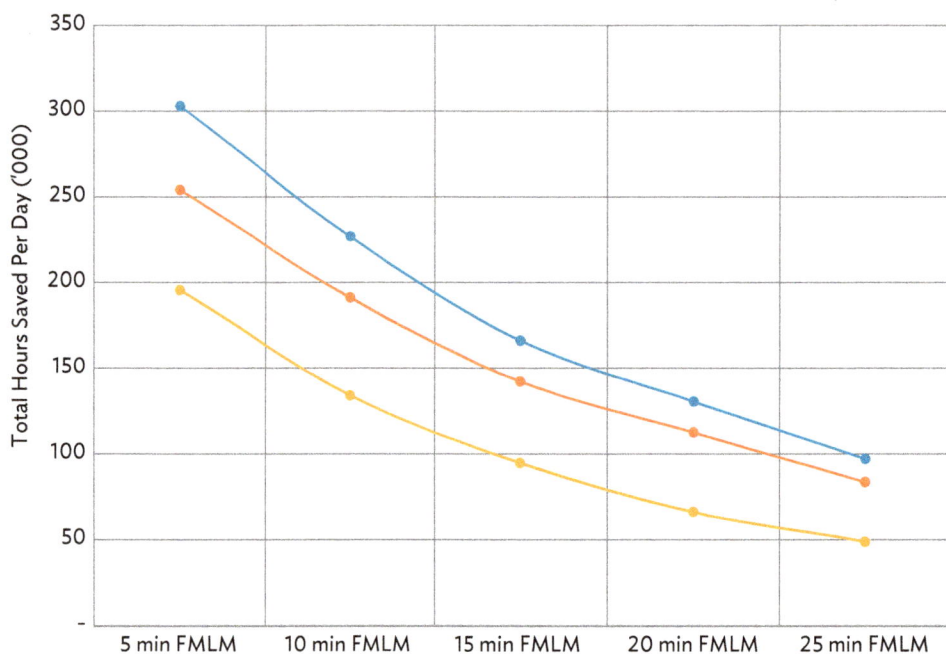

FAR = floor area ratio, FMLM = first mile and last mile, min = minute.
Source: World Resources Institute (WRI) India.

## Figure 21: Value of Time Sensitivity to First Mile and Last Mile Travel Times

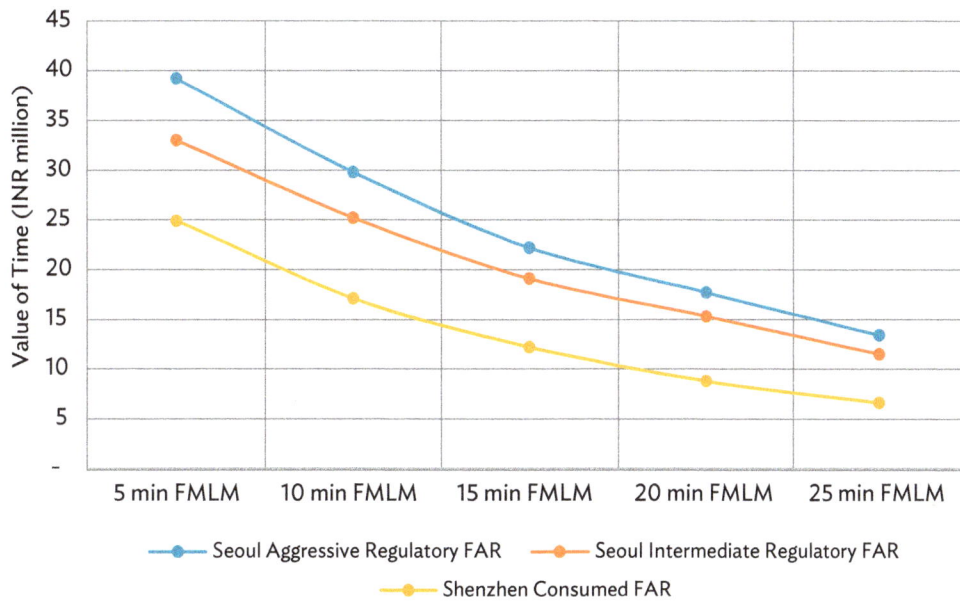

₹ = rupee, FAR = floor area ratio, FMLM = first mile and last mile, min = minute.
Source: World Resources Institute (WRI) India.

## Figure 22: Greenhouse Gas Emission Reduction Sensitivity to First Mile and Last Mile Travel Times

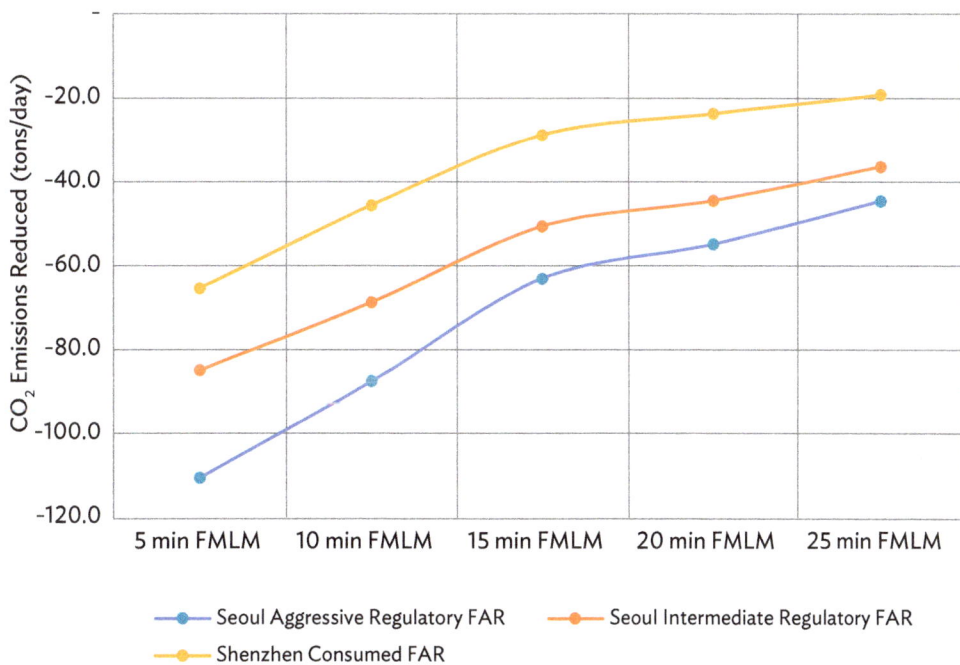

FAR = floor area ratio, FMLM = first mile and last mile, min = minute.
Source: World Resources Institute (WRI) India.

# Own-Source Revenue Generation

International best practice highlights the need to earmark revenue from LVC modes, among other non-fare box revenue sources for the metro rail. Doing so could increase the credit rating of metro projects, making them attractive debt options for investors, and provide an impetus for upgrading these networks in the long run. Table 25 shows the percentage increase of aggregate property value, (annual) property tax by residential and nonresidential floor space, and net profit by real estate developers under a simulated Seoul regulatory FAR scenario and a Shenzhen consumed FAR scenario, compared to the baseline scenarios.[14]

By relaxing the FAR, the city sees a 32%–40% increase in property values. After accounting for the increased unit construction cost of high-rises, the remaining increase in value, distributed among property tax revenue and net profit, should create a "win–win" situation for the public sector and real estate developers. In the simulations, the increase in additional property tax for residential floor space is 36%–39% and for nonresidential floor space it is 37%–51%; the net profit for real estate developers increases by 31%–42%.

Combining FAR relaxation and investment in the metro network results in an even higher increase in property value and associated distributions.[15] Property value increases by 34%–43%, property tax on residential floor space by 38%–41%, property tax on nonresidential floor space by 39%–55%, and net profit for real estate developers by 34%–45%.

### Table 25: Changes in Land Value, Property Taxes, and Profits
#### (%)

| Changes to Baseline | Seoul Regulatory FAR | Shenzhen Consumed FAR |
|---|---|---|
| **FAR relaxation** | | |
| Property value | 32 | 40 |
| Property tax residential | 36 | 39 |
| Property tax nonresidential | 51 | 37 |
| Net profit | 31 | 42 |
| **FAR Relaxation + Metro Investment** | | |
| Property value | 34 | 43 |
| Property tax residential | 38 | 41 |
| Property tax nonresidential | 55 | 39 |
| Net profit | 34 | 45 |

FAR = floor area ratio.

Source: World Resources Institute (WRI) India.

---

[14]   This analysis has been conducted for two simulations: Seoul intermediate regulatory FAR and consumed FAR of Shenzhen. It assumes perfect elastic floor space demand in the long run.

[15]   Based on a review of information on property value increases around metro stations in the Indian context, it is assumed that property values increase by 10%.

# Job Density and Wage Increase

The analysis now turns to exploring the extent of economic benefits, as captured by changes in job density and wages, that accrue to cities if the FAR is relaxed, and if this relaxation is combined with the presence of metro rail infrastructure. Ward-level attributes compiled from several sources, such as Census 2011 and Household Travel Survey data from RITES (2015), were used to perform econometric analysis of job density at the ward level in Bengaluru.[16]

The equation below was estimated by ordinary least squares (OLS) forward i:

Job density$_i$ = $b_0$ + $b_{1i}$ Graduates + $b_{2i}$ Homeowners + $b_{3i}$ Occupations in government + $b_{4i}$ Distance to work + $b_{5i}$ Commuters by car + $b_{6i}$ Commuters by two-wheelers + $b_{7i}$ Commuters by bus + $b_{8i}$ Commuters by bicycle + $b_{9i}$ Workforce participation rate + $b_{10i}$ FAR consumed + $b_{11i}$ Number of metro stations + $b_{12i}$ Slum population + $b_{13i}$ Nonresidential land use + $b_{14i}$ Road length + $b_{15i}$ Population density + $b_{16i}$ Open space + $e_i$

Table 26 defines the variables.

### Table 26: Econometric Analysis Variables

| Name | Measure |
|---|---|
| Graduates | Level of education: percentage of graduates |
| Homeowners | Home ownership: indicator of the permanence of residence |
| Occupations in government | Percent of workers employed in government |
| Distance to work | Indicator of job accessibility |
| Commuters by car | Commuting modality |
| Commuters by two-wheelers[a] | Commuting modality |
| Commuters by bus | Commuting modality |
| Commuters by bicycle | Commuting modality |
| Workforce participation rate | Workforce participation rate, part-time and full-time workers. |
| FAR consumed | FAR: Land use indicator |
| Number of metro stations | Number of metro stations: accessibility indicator |
| Slum population | Population living in slum |
| Nonresidential land use | Commercial or industrial land use |
| Road length | Road length |
| Population density | Density of population |
| Open space | Percentage of open space |

FAR = floor area ratio.

[a] The term "two-wheelers" in India refers mostly to two-wheel motorized vehicles (motorcycles, scooters, mopeds, etc.).

Source: Authors.

---

[16]  The analysis of this section is based on the background paper: K.S. Sridhar. 2020. *Economic Benefits of the Metro and Relaxed Land Use Regulations: Evidence from Bengaluru.*

When the OLS regression of job density on the FAR, the number of metro stations, and other controls is estimated, a sensitivity analysis of job density to variations in these "explanatory" variables—including the various scenarios of FARs detailed in the preceding sections—can be undertaken.[17] Four FAR simulations were analyzed to understand the extent of gains in job density. The first two scenarios are based on regulatory FARs (Intermediate Seoul FAR, Aggressive Seoul FAR), and the last two scenarios are based on the actual FAR consumed in Seoul and Shenzhen. The results from these scenarios are summarized in Table 27.

### Table 27: Density Gains Comparison from Counterfactual Floor Area Ratio Simulations

| | Seoul Intermediate Regulatory FAR | Seoul Aggressive Regulatory FAR | Shenzhen Consumed FAR |
|---|---|---|---|
| Average change in job density (jobs/ square kilometer) | 3,063 | 4,802 | 5,766 |

FAR = floor area ratio.
Source: Authors based on data from India Population Census 2011 and Rail India Technical and Economic Service Limited (RITES) Feasibility Report, 2015.

In parallel, the increase in average wages due to increased job density is considered. Based on a standard estimate of the elasticity of wage and density drawn from the urban economics—i.e., that a 1% increase in job density leads to a 0.05% increase in wages—it is possible to understand how much a relaxation of FAR contributes to increased wages, working via increases in job density and the exploitation of agglomeration benefits. Table 28 summarizes the increased wages across scenarios for FAR increases.

### Table 28: Summary of Wages Increases in Response to FAR Increases

| | Seoul Intermediate Regulatory FAR | Seoul Aggressive Regulatory FAR | Shenzhen Consumed FAR |
|---|---|---|---|
| Average increase in monthly wages (₹) | 16,308 | 29,380 | 15,290 |

₹ = rupees, FAR = floor area ratio.
Source: Authors based on data from India Population Census 2011 and Rail India Technical and Economic Service Limited (RITES) Feasibility Report, 2015.

Based on these results, it can be argued that relaxing land use regulations, specifically the FAR consumed, has a positive and favorable effect on wages. The wage increases are highest for the wards with the most aggressive increase in FARs.

## Caveats and Limitations

The data and methodology underlying the quantitative exercise of this chapter have several limitations. Remote sensing data, while providing superior coverage and granularity in measuring urban form than traditional survey data, has some gaps. The simulations involving changes in job density and their associated benefits are based on a set of simplifying assumptions based on "rules of thumb" drawn from the urban economics literature. For more realistic predictions, more rigorous spatial modelling and data are required. In addition, the following caveats are worth noting when interpreting the results of the foregoing quantitative exercise.

---

[17]   The estimates should be considered as reflecting correlations rather than causation. This is on account of several factors including the fact that the placement of metro stations is not random. To identify the casual relationship between FAR and metro placement on job density, further research is warranted.

(i)    In Bengaluru, built form is primarily regulated by plot sizes and the width of access roads, based on which maximum permissible ground coverage and FAR are stipulated, along with minimum setback requirements with respect to building height. For roads less than 9 m wide, the maximum building height permitted is 11.5 m. These building setback and height regulations hinder high-rise development and consumption of the maximum allowed FAR in several cases.

(ii)    In addition, other contextual and economic factors also affect the potential for full FAR consumption, such as the nature of existing construction and developments, potential and actual constraints on incremental additions, incentives for plot amalgamation and redevelopment, feasibility of upgrading infrastructure, and public and private capital available for investment. Furthermore, TOD implementation catering to higher density requires coordinated action across public sector agencies, for example, to shift underground utilities in TOD planning zones. Such actions place a burden on the concerned agencies.

(iii)    Based on the survey the WRI conducted at two metro stations, metro users spend 30–50 minutes on average for FMLM connectivity. Safe, fast, and efficient station area access is key for realizing the benefits estimated in the simulations. Increased densities could lead to increased congestion in the absence of efficient FMLM connectivity and prevent agglomeration benefits from being realized.

(iv)    Supportive policies, such as high parking charges within the TOD and metro catchment area and good infrastructure with safe and quick access to the metro stations, which encourage the shift from personal vehicles to metro, need to be implemented to reap the benefits of increased densities resulting from relaxed FAR.

(v)    The average pixel height data obtained from DLR WSF3D was helpful to compare the vertical profiles of the five cities. Higher resolution data, if available in the future, will help estimate realistic consumed FAR values and realistic counterfactual simulations. Parcel or lot and building footprint data, if available, would be even better for estimating accurate consumed FAR. The image in Figure 23 shows the limitation of the current pixel data. The red squares on the image are DLR WSF3D pixels and the aerial image is from Google Earth. The measured height of these buildings was around 60 m. The DLR pixel data on the left (Id–53240) has an average pixel height of 45 m and the adjacent pixel (Id–53241) has an average height of 19 m, even though the buildings in both pixels are the same height. As indicated before, the pixel height is the average of all the structures and open spaces inside it.

### Figure 23: DLR World Settlement Footprint Three-Dimensional Pixel Data Limitation

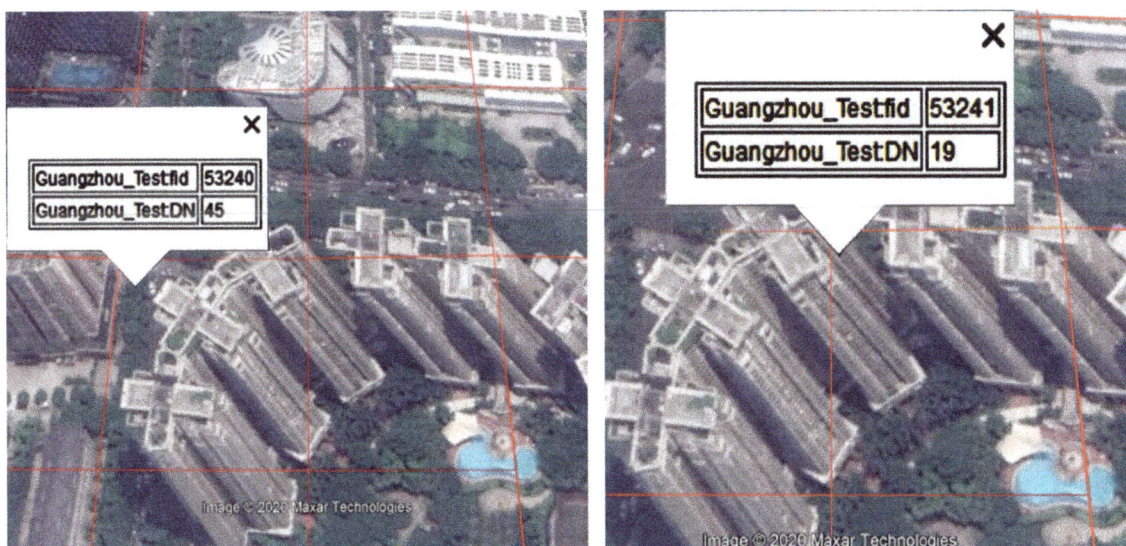

Source: World Resources Institute (WRI) India, based on Google Earth and Deutsches Zentrum für Luft- und Raumfahrt, German Aerospace Center (DLR) World Settlement Footprint (WSF) Three-Dimensional pixel data.

(vi)   The study team used land use data derived by applying machine-learning algorithms to satellite imagery. While this is useful, access to the official land use data for Bengaluru would be better.

(vii)   The quantitative analysis suggests several areas for future research. First, the impact of FAR relaxation on job density needs to be studied using a before-and-after method and comparing locations with varying FARs. Second, due to data limitations, the quantification of own-source revenue generation does not account for the potential difference in property value appreciation within the influence zones of metro stations compared to properties outside of the influence zones. Future research should quantify the impact of the metro network on LVC (within and outside influence zones) for decisions regarding sharing of revenue. Third, future research should examine heterogenous impacts of property value appreciation on different income groups and prescribe inclusive TOD solutions, such as affordable housing.

# 6 Final Remarks

Transit-oriented development (TOD) and land value capture can make significant contributions to the sustainability of large investments in mass transit systems, as well as the livability and economic dynamism of urban settlements. For the positive effects to be realized, however, requires establishing strong and effective planning, institutional, and financing frameworks.

Indeed, the qualitative analysis in this study finds that achieving the desired densification and development within transit influence zones is challenging. In particular, land use management is a critical factor that interacts with transit options and influences how cities evolve spatially. The particular set of land-related regulations and practices in place influence the nature of development within transit influence zones and have a bearing on the accessibility to jobs.

Extending this idea, the quantitative analysis of relaxing floor area ratio (FAR) restrictions in the Bengaluru metro corridor shows that the city's metro network could reap a multitude of economic gains. The key synergy between metro systems and land use policy stems from their combined effect on densification and its resulting impact on productivity and the labor market. Under various assumptions that draw upon the urban economics literature, among others, simulations of relaxed FAR demonstrate an increase in population densities, travel time savings, property values, and wages. They also show a reduction in carbon dioxide emissions. The results therefore suggest that appropriate land use regulations, coupled with appropriate TOD policies, would result in positive socioeconomic impacts and pave the way for successful implementation of land-based financing tools in relation to the metro rail projects. The policy implication extends beyond the case of Bengaluru. As the urbanization process in India continues, an increasing number of Indian cities are well on track to become mega cities. Preemptive planning of transport investment and land use management can go a long way to realize the potential of cities.

However, international practices show that these impacts can only be realized if strong and effective planning, institutional, and financing frameworks are established. Therefore, this three-pronged approach is essential to ensuring better utilization of TOD systems and to creating new financing mechanisms in India.

# APPENDIX
# Technical Data and Simulation Assumptions

## Estimating Average Consumed Floor Area Ratio for Bengaluru

Deutsches Zentrum für Luft- und Raumfahrt (DLR, German Aerospace Center) 90 meters (m) vertical density World Settlement Footprint Three-Dimensional (WSF3D) and imperviousness datasets were used for estimating the proxy average consumed floor area ratio (FAR) at the ward level. The process flowchart shown in Figure A1 identifies the steps used for estimating the average consumed FAR.

The three key assumptions that are critical to the process are as follows:

(i) **Average floor height (3.5 m).** This was based on Table 4.2 in the Model Building-Bye-laws of Bengaluru (http://mohua.gov.in/upload/uploadfiles/files/Chap-4.pdf) and observations on typical floor heights of apartments in Bengaluru.

(ii) **Road area ~30% of the built-up area.** This was derived using Bruhat Bengaluru Mahanagara Palika (BBMP) ward-level infrastructure attributes.

(iii) **Actual average FAR is ~1.1 times the FAR proxy computed.** This was derived by comparing the FAR calculated in an earlier World Resources Institute (WRI) study using the granular building footprint and lot size data for two stations in Bengaluru with the proxy FAR estimated using the 90 m DLR (WSF3D) data.

## Data and Assumptions for Simulations

To figure out the ideal FAR values for the simulations, we accounted for the developmental or regulatory guidelines for Bengaluru, Hyderabad, and Seoul.

**Representative regulatory FARs for Bengaluru.** The current Regional Master Plan (2015) for Bengaluru allows for a FAR of 4 within 150 m from a metro station for both residential and commercial developments. A FAR of 4 was used for simulating the ideal Bengaluru FAR scenario.

**Representative regulatory FARs for Hyderabad.** A FAR was not prescribed in the developmental regulations of Hyderabad. Equivalent floor space index (FSI) values were estimated based on the provisions in the development regulations. In general, equivalent FSI values ranged from 1.0 to 3.4 and for high-rise buildings, the FSI values ranged from 3 to 7. The average values for residential and nonresidential high-rise buildings were used for simulating the ideal Hyderabad FAR scenario.

# Figure A1: Proxy Average Consumed Floor Area Ratio Estimation Process Flowchart

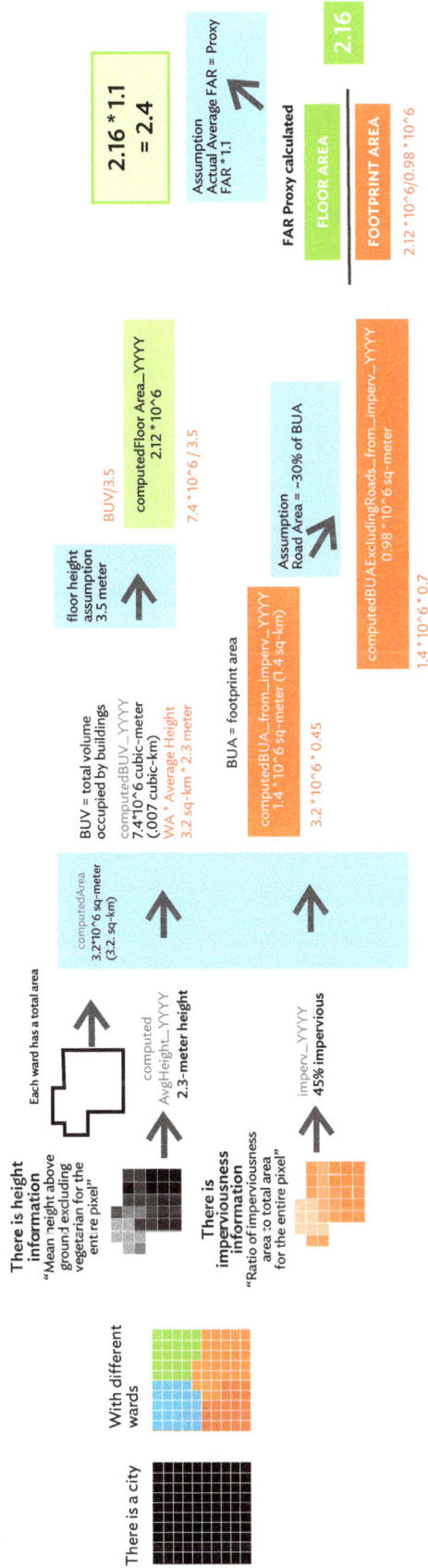

There is a city

With different wards

**There is height information**
"Mean height above ground excluding vegetation for the entire pixel"

Each ward has a total area

computed AvgHeight_YYYY
**2.3-meter height**

**There is imperviousness information**
"Ratio of imperviousness area to total area for the entire pixel"

imperv_YYYY
**45% impervious**

computedArea
3.2*10^6 sq-meter
(3.2 sq-km)

BUV = total volume occupied by buildings
computedBUV_YYYY
7.4*10^6 cubic-meter
(.007 cubic-km)
WA * Average Height
3.2 sq-km * 2.3 meter

BUA = footprint area

computedBUA_from_imperv_YYYY
1.4 * 10^6 sq-meter (1.4 sq-km)

3.2*10^6 * 0.45

floor height assumption
3.5 meter

BUV/3.5

computedFloor Area_YYYY
2.12*10^6

7.4 *10^6 / 3.5

**Assumption**
Road Area = ~30% of BUA

computedBUAExcludingRoads_from_imperv_YYYY
0.98 *10^6 sq-meter

1.4 *10^6 * 0.7

**2.16 * 1.1 = 2.4**

**Assumption**
Actual Average FAR = Proxy FAR * 1.1

FAR Proxy calculated

FLOOR AREA
**2.16**

FOOTPRINT AREA

2.12 *10^6/0.98 *10^6

BUA = built up area, BUV = built up volume, FAR = floor area ratio, sq km = square kilometer.

Source: World Resources Institute (WRI) India.

**Representative regulatory FARs for Seoul.** Most recent FAR values were not available for Seoul. Redevelopment projects implemented during 1976–2008 consumed an average FAR of 658%. The national FAR guidelines shown in Table A1 were available for the Republic of Korea. For residential developments, the maximum value of 5 under quasi-residential development, and for commercial developments, the maximum value of 13 under the "General" development type, were used to simulate ideal Seoul FAR values.

Various FARs are prescribed in the regulatory framework in the three cities depending on the land use, location, road width, and other factors. But the representative FARs selected for simulations are on the higher side and were selected to demonstrate the potential of how FAR relaxation can affect the density shifts.

### Table A1: National-Level Floor Area Ratio Regulations: Republic of Korea

| Area | Category | Description | LBR | FAR |
|------|----------|-------------|-----|-----|
| Residential | Class I exclusive | To protect residential environments for independent housing | 50 | 50–100 |
| | Class II exclusive | To protect residential environments for multi-unit housing | 50 | 100–150 |
| | Class I general | To create convenient residential environments for low-floor housing | 60 | 100–200 |
| | Class II general | To create convenient residential environments for mid-floor housing | 60 | 150–250 |
| | Class III general | To create convenient residential environments for mid/high-floor housing | 50 | 200–300 |
| | Quasi residential | To provide commercial environments to residential areas | 70 | 200–500 |
| Commercial | Central | To expand the commercial functions in the center/subcenter | 90 | 400–1,500 |
| | General | To provide general commercial and business functions | 80 | 300–1,300 |
| | Neighboring | To supply the daily necessities and services in the neighboring area | 70 | 200–900 |
| | Circulative | To increase the circulation function in the city and between the areas | 80 | 200–1,100 |
| Industrial | Exclusive | To admit the heavy chemical industry, pollutive industries, etc. | 70 | 150–300 |
| | General | To allocate industry not detrimental to the environment | 70 | 200–350 |
| | Quasi-industrial | To admit light industry and other industries, but in need of supplementing the residential, commercial functions | 70 | 200–400 |
| Green | Conservation | To protect natural environment and green areas in the city | 20 | 50–80 |

FAR = floor area ratio, LBR = land-to-building ratio.
Source: The Governance of Land Use in Korea. https://www.oecd-ilibrary.org/urban-rural-and-regional-development/the-governance-of-land-use-in-korea_fae634b4-en.

Table A2 shows the regulatory FAR values that were used in estimating the ward-level simulated FAR values.

### Table A2: Representative Floor Area Ratios Used in Counterfactual Simulations

| City | Simulated Residential FAR | Simulated Nonresidential FAR |
|---|---|---|
| Bengaluru | 4 | 4 |
| Hyderabad | 4 | 6 |
| Seoul | 5 | 13 |

FAR = floor area ratio.
Source: World Resources Institute (WRI) India.

The FAR values in Table A2 are not based on the actual consumed FAR in these cities. In some cases, the maximum permissible FAR based on the regulatory framework may not be completely consumed by a city. Therefore, ward-level simulated FARs representative of consumed FAR in international cities (Seoul and Shenzhen) were also estimated.

**Representative consumed FAR for Seoul.** The DLR pixel height data for Seoul are used as a proxy for consumed FAR. This is accomplished by adjusting the number of pixels in Bengaluru within the height bins >10 m and above by applying similar height bin proportions for Seoul.

**Representative consumed FAR for Shenzhen.** The DLR pixel height data for Shenzhen are used as a proxy for consumed FAR. This is accomplished by adjusting the number of pixels in Bengaluru within the height bins >10 m and above by applying similar height bin proportions for Seoul.

The second step was to apply these representative FARs to estimate simulated FAR values for each ward. The wards with metro coverage or catchment area, defined as the proportion of the ward area that falls within a 1 kilometer buffer of metro station(s), are assumed to benefit the most from FAR relaxation values shown in previous table. The location of the ward with respect to the Outer Ring Road (ORR) determines the extent of ward area expected to consume the new FAR values. The wards that lie inside the ORR, considered as core city, are mostly built out. Barring any urban redevelopment policies and priorities, these wards will have a hard time consuming higher FAR values. The wards that lie outside the ORR are less dense than the core city, have larger lot sizes, and can easily consume the higher FAR values. Two scenarios (Intermediate or Moderate Aggressive, Most Aggressive) with different sets of assumptions were developed for estimating the simulated FARs. In the first two scenarios, FAR relaxation is applied only to wards with metro coverage of > 25%. FAR relaxation is applied to all wards with metro coverage greater than zero. The detailed assumptions are documented below.

The FAR simulations and the respective analyses are based on a set of simplifying assumptions, aimed at comparing alternative scenarios and showcasing underlying mechanisms of transport and urban planning interactions, rather than creating hard predictions. The underlying assumption in all the simulations is that all three frameworks (planning, institutional, and financial) are established and functional as per the best practices.

**Intermediate scenario:** the following assumptions were used for the three FAR simulations under the intermediate scenario:

(i)  For wards with metro coverage > 25% and outside the ORR: 25% of the ward area is assumed to consume the simulated FAR values.

(ii)  For wards with metro coverage > 25% and inside ORR: 10% of the ward area is assumed to consume the simulated FAR values.

(iii)  If none of the preceding conditions are met: No new simulated FAR is consumed in the ward.

**Aggressive scenario:** the following assumptions were used for the three FAR simulations under the aggressive scenario:

(i)     for wards with metro coverage > 0% and outside the ORR: 100% of the area within a 150 m radius consumes the simulated FAR plus 25% of rest of ward consumes the simulated FAR;

(ii)    for wards with metro coverage > 0% inside ORR: 100% of area within a 150 m radius consumes the simulated FAR plus 10% of rest of ward consumes simulated FAR; and

(iii)   if none of the preceding conditions are met: no new simulated FAR is consumed in the ward

## Ward-Level Floor Area Ratio Simulation Based on Regulatory Floor Area Ratios in Peer Cities

Under each scenario, ward-level simulated FARs were generated by applying regulatory FAR values of Bengaluru, Hyderabad, and Seoul. This resulted in nine different simulated ward-level FAR values. The following steps were used to calculate the new simulated FARs.

(i)     Because different FARs for residential and commercial use are being simulated for Hyderabad and Seoul, the first step was to estimate the amount of residential and nonresidential areas that will be consuming the new simulated FARs by applying the respective scenario assumptions.

(ii)    The second step was to estimate new simulated FARs for each ward. This was estimated by applying a weighted average to the portion of the ward where new FAR values will be applied to the rest of the unaffected ward area.

## Ward-Level Floor Area Ratio Simulation Based on Consumed Floor Area Ratios in Peer Cities

This simulation is done by utilizing DLR pixel height data. The pixel height data are used as the proxy for consumed FAR. The proportion of pixels in bins taller than 10 m for Bengaluru is adjusted to reflect the distribution of pixels in peer cities (Seoul and Shenzhen). The following series of steps were used to simulate FARs based on consumed FARs in peer cities.

(i)     Estimate the number of pixels by bin height in Bengaluru for bins taller than 10 m for which the heights need to be adjusted so the distribution is similar to that of a peer city. Stratify the count of these pixels to be adjusted into two groups (inside and outside the metro catchment area).

(ii)    Sort the pixels in Bengaluru first by station or non-station status, followed by descending order of the pixel heights.

(iii)   Based on the counts estimated in step (i), adjust the height of the pixels to follow the distribution in each bucket of the respective peer city (Seoul, Shenzhen).

(iv)    Aggregate new height at the ward level.

(v)     Estimate the new ward-level FARs based on the new average height of the wards.

Table A3 summarizes the base and new FAR average values resulting from all the regulatory and consumed FAR simulations. Some of the key observations are as follows:

(i)   Wards inside the ORR consumed higher FARs than the ones outside. The average base FAR for all BBMP wards is 1.90. The average base FAR for wards inside the ORR is 2.06 and outside the ORR is 1.57. Wards inside the ORR consumed higher FARs than the ones outside.

(ii)  The new average FAR for all BBMP wards ranges from 2.08 to 2.80. Of all the simulations based on regulatory FAR values, the intermediate scenario simulation based on the Bengaluru FAR has the lowest increase at 9.5%, and the most aggressive scenario simulation based on the Seoul FAR has the highest increase at 40.0%. The simulation based on Shenzhen consumed FAR resulted in a 47.4% increase in the average FAR.

(iii) The wards outside the ORR experienced a higher increase in the average FAR than the ones inside for all the simulations based on regulatory FAR values. In contrast, the wards inside the ORR experienced the higher increase in the average FAR for the simulations based on the consumed FAR. This is because of the difference in assumptions and methodology used for simulations.

### Table A3: High-Level Comparative Simulated Floor Area Ratio Changes

| Scenario | Intermediate Bengaluru Regulatory FAR | Intermediate Hyderabad Regulatory FAR | Intermediate Seoul Regulatory FAR | Aggressive Bengaluru Regulatory FAR | Aggressive Hyderabad Regulatory FAR | Aggressive Seoul Regulatory FAR | Shenzhen Consumed FAR |
|---|---|---|---|---|---|---|---|
| Affected Wards | 118 | 118 | 118 | 161 | 161 | 161 | 186 |
| Pct Affected Wards | 60% | 60% | 60% | 81% | 81% | 81% | 94% |
| Average Base BBMP FAR | 1.9 | 1.9 | 1.9 | 1.9 | 1.9 | 1.9 | 1.9 |
| New Average BBMP FAR | 2.08 | 2.13 | 2.38 | 2.19 | 2.27 | 2.65 | 2.8 |
| Percent Change | 9.50% | 12.10% | 25.30% | 15.30% | 19.50% | 39.50% | 47.40% |
| Average Base FAR Inside ORR | 2.06 | 2.06 | 2.06 | 2.06 | 2.06 | 2.06 | 2.06 |
| Average Base FAR Outside ORR | 1.57 | 1.57 | 1.57 | 1.57 | 1.57 | 1.57 | 1.57 |
| New Average FAR Inside ORR | 2.18 | 2.22 | 2.39 | 2.25 | 2.31 | 2.58 | 3.23 |
| New Average FAR Outside ORR | 1.88 | 1.96 | 2.34 | 2.07 | 2.2 | 2.79 | 1.95 |
| Pct FAR change inside ORR | 5.80% | 7.80% | 16.00% | 9.20% | 12.10% | 25.20% | 56.80% |
| Pct FAR Change Outside ORR | 19.70% | 24.80% | 49.00% | 31.80% | 40.10% | 77.70% | 24.20% |

BBMP = Bruhat Bengaluru Mahanagara Palika, FAR = floor area ratio, ORR = Outer Ring Road.
Source: DLR Pixel height data, World Resources Institute (WRI) India.

www.ingramcontent.com/pod-product-compliance
Lightning Source LLC
Chambersburg PA
CBHW061221270326
41926CB00032B/4809